# Arabia

## - CHARLESTON'S -
## RED SEA PIRATES OF 1692

### BEING THE TRUE TALE OF CAPT. GEORGE RAYNOR & THE CREW OF THE BACHELOR'S DELIGHT

*The history, origins, and occurrence surrounding Charleston's "Red Sea Men," also known as "The Privateers," of the Loyal Jamaica - formerly Bachelor's Delight.*

By Adam Morrow, alias Captain Marrow

Printed by KDP Publishing, 2025

**Editor:** Ava Lin Pence
**Cover Design by:** Adam Morrow
**Cover and Interior Design Art Credits:**

Van der Aa, Pieter, *Map of the Arabian Peninsula and Red Sea*, 1706.
>https://commons.wikimedia.org/wiki/File:Pieter_van_der_Aa_-_map_of_Red_Sea.jpg.
CC-PD-Mark

Scott, Samuel, *Capture du galion espagnol Nuestra Señora de Covadonga par le navire britannique Centurion, commandé par George Anson, le 20 juin 1743.*
>https://commons.wikimedia.org/wiki/File:Samuel_Scott_1.jpg, PD-old-100-expired

Roux, George, *Long John Silver Finding the Skeleton*, 1929. CC-PD-Mark, PD-old-80-expired

"Old Leather Book," enginemonkey, deviantart.com, 2010 [1640]

The Fell Types are digitally reproduced by Igino Marini and used with
>permission. www.iginomarini.com.

"Gold Mohur of Mughal Emperor Aurangzeb, Minted at Multan" & "Gold Coin of Sulemain the Magnificent, Struck at the Cairo Mint" each by user LouisAragon, 2019, 2022. Accessed:
>https://commons.wikimedia.org/wiki/File:Gold_mohur_of_Mughal_Emperor_Aurangzeb,_minted_at_Multan.jpg, and
>https://commons.wikimedia.org/wiki/File:Gold_coin_of_Suleiman_the_Magnificent,_struck_at_the_Cairo_mint.jpg, each cropped and used as per the Creative Commons Attribution-Share Alike 2.5 Generic License:
>https://commons.wikimedia.org/wiki/Commons:GNU_Free_Documentation_License,_version_1.2

"a Ahlan Wasahlan" by wep, used with permission for personal & Commercial purpose.
"Booter" by Apostrophic Lab, used with permission for personal & Commercial purpose.
"Captain Marrow Skull & Bones," Adam Morrow, 2021
**Layout & Design by:** Adam Morrow

This publication is not to be reproduced in any form, by any electronic or physical means, without explicit written permission of the copyright owner.

ISBN 9798312929218

Text Copyright © 2025 by Adam Morrow. All rights reserved.

*"Commerce has set the mark of selfishness,
The signet of its all-enslaving power
Upon a shining ore, and called it gold:
Before whose image bow the vulgar great,
The vainly rich, the miserable proud,
The mob of peasants, nobles, priests, and kings.
...Gold is a living god and rules in scorn,
all earthly things but virtue."*

- "Queen Mab, Book V," Percy Bysshe Shelley, 1813

# ACKNOWLEDGEMENTS

I would like to dedicate this book to Ava Lin Pence. Who would have thought that after growing up along the Treasure Coast of Florida, and a life-long fascination of Spanish shipwreck treasure, that you'd end up with a pirate? Between finding you and pirate history; moving to Charleston so many years back wasn't such a bad thing. You've never once doubted me, and have instead supported and assisted me every step of the way. Like a seagull loves a french fry handout; I love you.

# TABLE OF CONTENTS

FOREWORD............................................................... 11

CHAPTER ONE:
SETTING THE STAGE........................................ 13
- The Mutiny............................................................ 18

CHAPTER TWO:
RISE OF THE BACHELOR'S DELIGHT.............. 21
- The Mughal Empire............................................... 25
- Capture of a Lifetime............................................ 27

CHAPTER THREE:
THE VOYAGE HOME........................................... 37

CHAPTER FOUR:
CHARLES TOWNE, SOUTH CAROLINA.............. 53

CHAPTER FIVE:
THE RED SEA MEN LEGACY............................... 69
- Analysis of Captain George Raynor..................... 76
- Public Reception.................................................. 81

CHAPTER SIX:
THE MUDDLED MESS & MISCONCEPTIONS..... 85
- George / Josiah Raynor........................................ 85
- James Kelly's Deposition..................................... 54
- Bachelor's Delight & Batchelor's Delight............. 54
- Local Folklore of the Loyal Jamaica.................... 54

EPILOGUE.................................................................. 311

SOURCES................................................................... 311

INDEX......................................................................... 311

7

LIST OF FIGURES.................................................. 311

ABOUT THE AUTHOR........................................ 351

*"A Frigate at Sea,"* by Pierre Puget (1620-1694)

# FOREWORD

Ahoy reader! Before you is, as the book's name implies, the summarized account of Charleston's Red Sea Men, the pirates that came to this harbor in the spring of 1692 ~ a long-adored topic of mine. I would first like to thank you for taking your time to find an interest in my written work, and would also like to dislcose that the contents of this history book are a mixture of recorded facts stemming from primary sources - the problems that arise from them, and concluding with my own speculative thoughts on the evidence we do have. I will surely note to you the reader when I step aside and discuss possibilities. This book has been a long-time coming for me, as when I relocated to Charleston in 2006 from South Haven, Michigan, it admittedly took me some time to latch onto something here to admire of my "new home." This ultimately ended up being pirate history, through which I've already had quite the adventure myself. While tales of Blackbeard and Bonnet dominate our Carolinian coasts, I found myself drawn to "privateer" George Raynor and his men, the obscurity of the event, and how it has since been seemingly "swept under the rug" by Charleston's portrayal of history, and what they instead opt to capitalize on with their representation of the city's history. Raynor and the Red Sea Men are, as far as I'm concerned, a very rich and adventurous element of history that is worth telling, and that very few know.

    I will note that through collaboration with fellow pirate historian and author, Matt McClaine, the agreed upon narrative that makes the most sense is that of a collection of research assembled by Reynald Laprise, a skilled French scholar and historian. The history presented in this book operates on the premise that this is the most sound timeline and events, though it is of course compounded and elaborated upon by my own research into primary documents and geneology work, done by myself and those of the descendents of the Raynor family.

*Arabian Gold: Charleston's Red Sea Pirates of* 1692

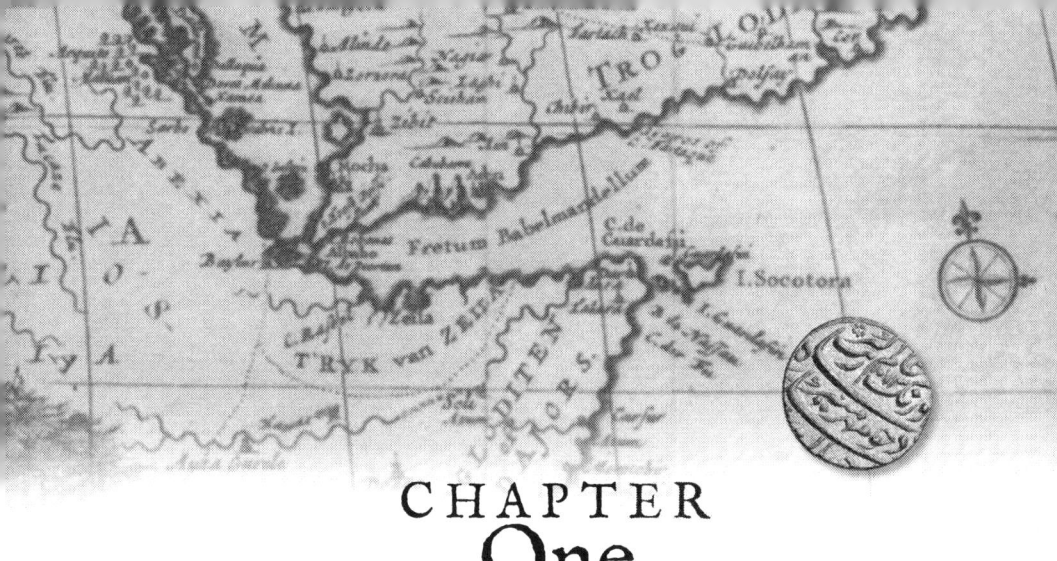

# CHAPTER
# One

### *Port Royal, Jamaica - Setting the Stage*

The adventure of the pirate crew of the *Bachelor's Delight* begins in the year 1690, before *Bachelor's Delight* enters the picture, at Port Royal, Jamaica. This is a time of war, pitting the countries of England against France in the Nine Years War, or the War of the Grand Alliance, stretching from 1688 to 1697. England however wasn't alone in this fight, allied with the Holy Roman Empire, the Dutch Republic, Spain, Savoy, Sweden, and a variety of German states, the alliance fought against those owing allegiance to King Louis the 16th.[1] The conflict erupted as a result of France's king pushing for expansion, the shockwave of which would be felt as far as the Caribbean, and would continue to do so for some time. For even upon its conclusion in 1697 it only led to the War of Spanish Succession, or Queen Anne's War, in 1701. That war of which would lead many sailors to careers as legal seafaring privateers, who would afterwards turn to piracy and where many of the most famous names in pirate history originate. As for Port Royal in 1690, the conflict with France saw two of the most famous "pirate ports" of all time against each other - England's Port Royal, notorious for its history of piracy and debauchery, and the French buccaneer island of Tortuga off the northwestern shore of Hispanola, or modern-day Haiti, across from Port de Paix.

Extending out into the Kingston Harbor of Jamaica, Port Royal functioned essentially as a capitol of sorts, rivaling the imports and exports with the American port of Boston, Massachusetts.

(**Figure 1**: *Cropped "Map Showing the Harbours of Port Royal and Kingston, Jamaica," by Edward Long, 1774*)

Famously the port is 'adoringly' remembered within pirate history as "the richest and wickedest city in the world" by many back home in England, noting the cesspool of piracy, smuggling, crime, and the port's amount of brothels and drinking establishments allegedly outnumbering residential homes and honest businesses. A modern day "Sodom" to the folks of the 17th century, from their outside perspective back in England. To those partaking in the riches and hedonism offered by Port Royal, it was wonderful. It is from here that the Brethren of the Coast had once previously operated in the 1660s; a coalition of pirates operating from both here and Tortuga, long before the Nine Years War.[2] It is here too that the famous Captain Henry Morgan launched fleets of privateers against the Spanish Main, and for a time was even appointed governor before his death in 1688, just one year before our story begins.

As the year of 1689 drew to a close, great concern of French vessels were a forefront thought by those of Port Royal, especially after a series

*Port Royal, Jamaica - Setting the Stage*

(**Figure 2**: *"View of Port Royal and Kingston Harbours," by Edward Long, 1774)*

of raids enacted upon Jamaica's shores by a Dutch pirate named Laurens de Graaf. Working on behalf of France, de Graaf was an experienced individual who had been on the account, that is, to be pirating, for nearly fifteen years before this point - an impressive feat as this line of work often sees much smaller numbers before these seafarers typically meet a grisly fate or a hempen noose. He of course spent some of this time working legally as a privateer and even pirate-hunting, but as the year of 1690 was on the cusp of arrival, he and his men began plundering English ships and English plantations. While he would move on, away from Port Royal and to the Cayman Islands, on the 14th of October, the Council of Jamaica put forth plans to establish an armed guard sloop that would work to ensure the safety of Jamaica's fishing fleet. In December, another ship would be armed and join the first - but this was only the beginning.[3] Come February, 1690, it was decided upon that to combat the French foe, letters of marque would be issued to interested sailors, to any wishing to sail against France and plunder her vessels legally - as far as England would be concerned.[4] This can also be seen as a document issued for what some could consider "legal piracy," however there were often stipulations regarding their methods of capture and how spoils plundered were to be divided, the issuing nation of course not without wanting a cut themselves. This is privateering. In this scenario, willing sailors would agree upon and receive a legally binding document allowing them to plunder and capture French, and only French, vessels. Upon capture, the ship would need to be brought back to port for it to be inspected and documented; admittedly a bit more "red tape" so to speak than the prospect of piracy. Of course, to the opposing force you were still a foe all the same, supplied with a fancy piece of paper or not. These English privateers were functionally no different to the French than any other pirates, much in the same way many English privateers were viewed by Spain both before and after, and the same as how England felt about French Capitaine Laurens de Graaf.

In March, 1690, two Jamaican sloops would depart Port Royal as legal privateers. The sloop *Dyamond* (or *Diamond*), under the command of Captain Thomas Harrison, and the sloop *Mary*, captained by George Austen, and amid her crew a sailor named George Raynor. Seeing as how we are first now addressing this man, do note that many period documents portray his last name as Rayner, but also other less common alternate spellings such as Rainer, Reiner, and even Reigner. In modern times, the name has evolved to Raynor with the 'o' as the agreed upon spelling that history has largely gone with, much like Blackbeard's name of "Edward Teach" despite the original spellings. For simplicity's sake and cohesion throughout this work, going forward I will continue using this spelling of Raynor. These ships, sloops, were shallow-draft vessels that allowed for the navigation of shallow waters, such as many bays, shoals, coral reef, and inland waterways - and as a result they were often favored by pirates of the period. This allowed them to reliably pursue prey who would otherwise flee inland to escape, or for evasion themselves inland against pursuing naval vessels that rode lower in the water. These sloops set sail, bound for Santo Domingo. This endeavor would bring them to discovering a French ship to assault located not far offshore from Port de Paix; a bustling French port established long prior by French buccaneers out of nearby Tortuga just offshore. A discharge of gunpowder rocked the *Dyamond* as she fired at their target causing it to flee. *Mary*, however, had been positioned to give chase and saw the capture occur. This ship was *La Constance*, a 130 ton vessel that had previously sailed out from La Rochelle, France, under the captaincy of Pierre Thomas.[5] There is reason to believe that she may have possibly been a French frigate, based on an account we'll address later by a man named Adam Baldridge who goes on record regarding the specifications of the ship later, but could have reasonably also been a ketch. With her

## Port Royal, Jamaica - Setting the Stage

*(**Figure 3**: "Vue de la ville du Port de Paix," by Nicolas Ponce & Nicolas Ozanne, 1791)*

crew subdued, and the ship now in the hands of the English privateers, *La Constance* was hauled back down to Port Royal where she was inspected, as was part of the legal process of her capture. She was deemed a *"good catch,"* and purchased by John Bell & Company.[6] While Bell retained ownership of the vessel, the crew of the *Dyamond* and *Mary* were allowed to take her out for continued sailing against France, and the vessel was re-named to the *"Loyal Jamaica"* with Thomas Harrison of the *Dyamond* put in charge as her captain. It is likely that in addition to the crown taking a cut of any acquired booty they may accumulate going forward, contained within the legal records of Bell & Co. in Jamaica likely included a further stipulation of a cut for himself of what the sailors may, legally, capture with his ship. The *Loyal Jamaica* sailed away from Port Royal once more some time after May 31st, this time with Captain Harrison holding a new letter of marque for her, issued by the newly-arrived governor, The Earl of Inchiquin, William O'Brien.

# THE MUTINY

This is where the crew comes to a disagreement... particularly, the adherance to their legal commision, enforced by the lawful Captain Harrison while amid his men who had been mostly consolidated to the new *Loyal Jamaica*. The men had grown rather swayed to the opinion that a Spanish ship in their whereabouts had been ripe for the taking.. However, Spain were their allies, easy pickings or not, and accosting them would certainly invalidate the terms of their letter of marque. Doing so would seem them being irrevocably deemed pirates - traitors to England and to the Grand Alliance. It is for this reason, Harrison's stalwart opinion to not turn pirate, that a mutiny arose upon the ship. There is no mention this was any bloody conflict, and was likely a voting process with Harrison conceding to their wishes and opting to bow out of the crew. However the event unraveled, this saw the captain put ashore and degraded. With Harrison stripped of his captaincy and now out of the picture, it is at this point that many believe crewmate George Raynor was elected and put into this role. Yet another possible person put into this position of power prior to Raynor is that of a man named "Guillen," which is believed to have been James Gilliam - a pseudonym for a prominent figure of pirate history, James Kelly.

Kelly, by this time, had been deemed "an old buccaneer," who had found himself in Jamaica following the conclusion of his time spent sailing the South Seas under Captain Edward Davis; a grand voyage which was well-documented by William Dampier in his 1697 book *A New Voyage Round the World*, which to this day remains a great primary source from which we use to glean important information about how a period pirate crew functioned, as recorded by someone on the inside rather than newspaper or naval reports, which at times were designed to alarm the public and demonize these seafaring criminals. To jump far ahead, James Kelly would die nine years later, sentenced to death in England for his piratical crimes, and his single deposition left behind only a day before he faced the gallows presents unique information relevant to the story of Raynor and the *Loyal Jamaica*. In this deposition of Kelly, he relays that he for a time had been established as captain of their ship throughout her pirate activities off the western coast of Africa.[7] This accusation of a "Guillen" as captain after the mutiny comes from the commander of the Jamaican convoy, after October. Regardless of who was elected captain first, it was also at this

*Port Royal, Jamaica - Setting the Stage*

time the ship would be re-named once more.[8] Yet it should be noted this is not direct confirmation this was Kelly, that Kelly on his deathbed was telling the truth, and it should be acknowledged that most all other sources exclusively state it was Captain Raynor in charge at this time. But had Kelly truly been aboard, he likely would have been the more experienced of the two, but we don't exactly know why Raynor would end up ultimately as captain, for which merits. There is a strong possibilty however, that Raynor himself had already acquired a bit of experience himself as a seaman based on his age. According to Charleston records later in 1692, Raynor had been thirty-four years of age, meaning that if he'd been to sea intially as a young man in his late teens, as is often the case, he would easily have about a decade of experience aboard ships, if not more. Another claim states that Raynor was put in charge, with Kelly being assigned the role of quartermaster, essentially acting as supervisor.[9] Captain Raynor is generally known as entering history for the first time at this moment, with his life beforehand a mystery, not unlike so many other pirates throughout this period. There are allegations that Raynor originally had arrived to the Caribbean out of New York, but there are complications there that will be addressed later when acknowledging and analyzing his descendants and their geneological research. Yet conflicting this is the claim by Kelly that upon departure from Port Royal, he had instead taken a number of men aboard the *Dyamond* and parted ways to engage in his own escapades before later reconvening, or he commanded the *Dyamond* and potentially sailed in consort with the mutineers and their vessel. This will be addressed later when we analyze Kelly's potential involvement in greater detail.

On October 15th, the put-ashore and deposed Captain Thomas Harrison would finally arrive and deliver news of the mutineers, leading to a proclamation issued by Jamaica advocating for the apprehension of their vessel and capture of the renegades of the *Loyal Jamaica*.[10] However, word had not yet reached Port Royal of the newest name that the mutinous crew bestowed upon her. She was now a pirate vessel and armed with fourteen cannon - *Bachelor's Delight*.

*Arabian Gold: Charleston's Red Sea Pirates of* 1692

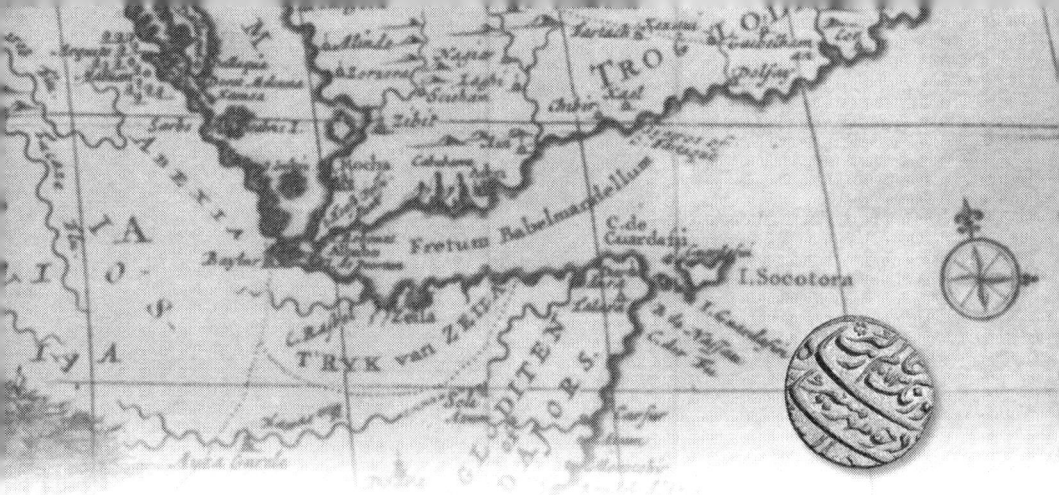

# CHAPTER
# Two

## *Rise of the Bachelor's Delight*

As names go regarding pirate ships, *Bachelor's Delight* certainly ranks high in what we can imagine to be an exciting pirate ship. But why did they choose it? *Loyal Jamaica* is really no mystery or head-scratcher. She had been a French ship, commandeered by English privateers out of Port Royal, loyal to Jamaica, admittedly albeit shortly. Perhaps the most simple answer is out of admiration or acknowledgement to the successful pirate vessel of Edward Davis of the aforementioned South Sea adventures - the slightly differently spelled *Batchelor's Delight*, coincidentally a 14 gun ship (yet other sources state she had been outfitted with 40 guns), that James Kelly had for a time been associated. Relevant in the scenario that we assume Kelly to be thoroughly involved in Raynor's tale. Multiple ships bearing the same name, even around the same time period or even the same area are certainly not unheard of. The amount of ships named Revenge are plentiful, as is the name popular name Adventure. Even the name Fancy would be used by both Henry Every in 1696, and by Edward Low nearly two decades later, which also is often thought to be a nod to Every's piratical success during his days. Even naval ships with seemingly very unique names are subject to this, such as HMS *Winchelsea*, also spelled *Winchelsey* often, of which there were five ships bearing this same name between 1694 and 1763, and more beyond that. It is speculated by author John Millar, that Kelly and the crew of Edward Davis titled their acquired ship *Batchelor's Delight* many years prior simply due to them being unwed, but also postulates that many of their crew had been intelligent and had been graduates prior, but this is not elaborated on. For what it's worth, "Bachelor's Delight" is also amusingly a modern slang title for an easy-to-create cheap meal. Until we return to touch upon the topic again later, we'll temporarily shelve this other former *Batchelor's Delight* of the 1680s.

Once the chain of command had been shaken up violently, and the crew now officially criminal mutineers, it was time to take the *Bachelor's Delight* and use her as the crew pleased, no longer adhering to the privateering commision drafted for the *Loyal Jamaica*, presumably tucked away in the captain's cabin, and siezed from Harrison. Their initial destination; The Canary Islands, or, the "Canaries." Located off the coast of Morocco in the Atlantic along northwestern Africa, the whereabouts of these volcanic isles would put the mutineers far away from England's conflict in the Caribbean, and far from Port Royal. The Canaries were, and still are, a community asset of Spain, and long-remained a popular destination for pirates. Not for those seeking a warm welcome, but merchant ships were plentiful, each loaded with bountiful plunder. These isles, diverse in geography, were very important to Spain and many years prior become a well-known primary stop along almost all ships' routes due to the north-east trade winds. They were also a very large exporter of cultivated sugarcane and imports of enslaved Africans, and the Canaries saw most of their business regarding voyages across the Atlantic back to Spanish ports in the West Indies; such as Havana.[1] The prominent wealth of the Canaries seemingly invited all manner of assault for them over the prior hundred years, and not just by pirates, but also from legal privateers from warring nations, and before them even by the Ottoman Empire. It was here amid these islands, the crew of the *Bachelor's Delight* assumedly assaulted the Spaniards, as was the aforementioned goal of some of her crew that of course resulted in the replacement of Captain Harrison. According to the tale of James Kelly, they would happen upon the ship *Vice Consul*, which the pirates would detain as a prisoner vessel, and for some time contemplated assaulting a port town of the isles, but opted to not follow through with the idea.[2] Once complete in the archipelago, the *Bachelor's Delight* set sail southward, bound for the Cape Verde Islands, about a thousand-miles south along Africa's coast.

Volcanic in formation as well, the white sandy beaches and rugged green mountains of the beautiful Cape Verde isles would next welcome the pirates; and once again, they would not be the first of their kind. Like the Canaries, the Cape Verde isles were a big attractent to piracy due to them being a major hub of the transatlantic slave trade. While considered an atrocity in our modern age, during the 1690s this simply meant to most seafarers that the isles were exporting highly valuable cargo, acting as a valuable waystation for enslaved peoples from Guinea-Bissau along the African coast to the south, to the rest of the Portuguese empire. At the time that the crew of the *Bachelor's Delight* made their way into the archipelago, the lower islands were currently still recovering from the disasterous eruption of the volcano Pico do Fogo on the island of Fogo, which occurred just a decade prior, and resulting in mass emigration of its people to the nearby island of Brava. According to the deposition of James Kelly, it was here that they plundered a Portuguese ship sitting in the harbor of Sao Tiago, who had been prepared to depart for Brazil. After a brief visit to Fogo, and then dumping the Portuguese prisoners off at Brava, the pirates set sail south following the African coast bound for the East Indies.

While their route would take them along a very prominent shipping route hugging along

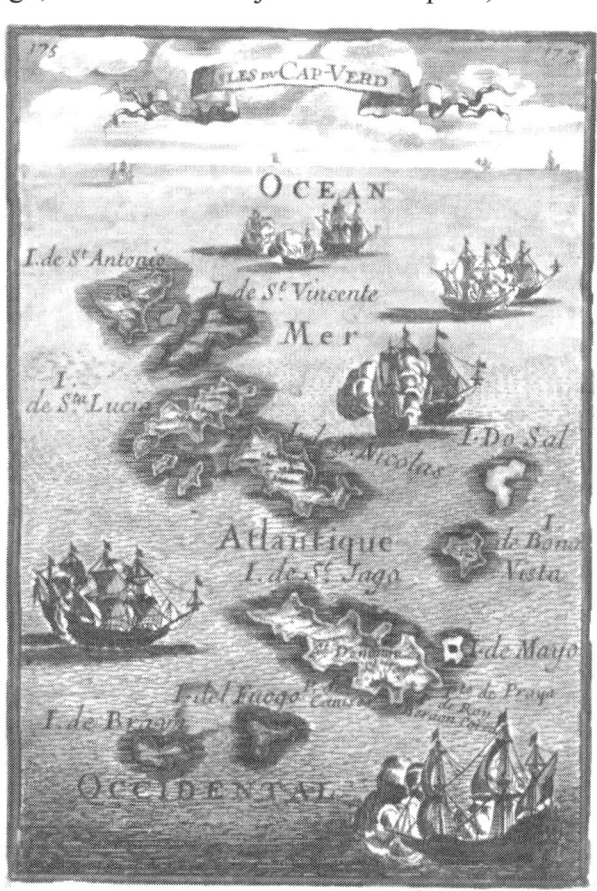

(**Figure 4**: *"Map of the Cape Verde Islands, 1683," by Alain Manesson Mallet*)

Africa's coast, particularly the exports of enslaved Africans shipped out from the Gold Coast, from European establishments such as those in Ghana, and Whydah, they would also happen upon incoming ships from the Indian Ocean having rounded the Cape of Good Hope near Africa's southern tip. These ships were delivering exports from the Red Sea, the Arabian peninsula, and valuables from the powerful Mughal Empire that currently dominated most of the Indian subcontinent who had established a heavy focus on nautical trade. While likely presented with numerous tempting options along their journey south, there are no recorded assaults made by the pirate crew along this route. It's not uncommon for small piratical assaults to go unheard of or going unreported. Many times merchant captains were simply delivering cargo from one company to another, with the cargo loaded aboard not necessarily their own personal wares - but they would be held responsible for its well-being and security. There have been noted occasions where merchant captains would rather take the loss of plundered goods out of their own pocket than report that they allowed the cargo to be taken away by robbers. It can be speculated that in addition to the other noted ships hit by the *Bachelor's Delight* there may have been smaller incidents as well, but again, this would be pure speculation.

As for the destination the pirates would next reach, it remains partially in question, primarily from the issues that arise from James Kelly's notes, but for now we'll assume that their route took them past the Cape of Good Hope and up through the Mozambique Channel that seperates the African shores, such as Somalia's, from the large island of Madagascar. Once through the Channel, and after passing the island of Socatra, the pirates found themselves arriving to the Gulf of Aden in August, 1691. The crew were about to engage in what would be considered "Red Sea piracy," an endeavor they would go on to successfully complete, and Raynor's men would go on to set an example of what could be achieved for pirates in the coming years by those who would follow in their footsteps, such as Thomas Tew and Henry Every. Lucrative piratical trips such as these to the Red Sea and then back to the Americas would become popularized by history as "the Pirate Round."

*Rise of the Bachelor's Delight*

## RED SEA PIRACY

Along the southeastern shores of Madagascar, the French port of Fort Dauphin would be constructed, many years before the crew of the *Bachelor's Delight* would arrive to these parts of the world, in 1643 to be precise. It had been named in honor of Louis the 16th of France, despite him being but a child at this period. This was the first settlement on the island by France, which eventually would fall after relations with the native Antonosy people went south during 1674. Eventually, this did of course lead to a variety of French, as well as Danish, pirates who had become familiar with the waters and proceeded to plunder the Arabian Sea and Indian Ocean during the 1680s. As such, the *Bachelor's Delight* would hardly be the first pirates to consider heading to these waters - but they were the first of pirates from the Americas to cross the Atlantic, follow the coastline of Africa, assault ships out of the Red Sea, and then return home in possession of much foreign wealth for their efforts. This would quickly become the example of the aforementioned Pirate Round; a piratical voyage out to the Red Sea, typically departing out of either Jamaica or Boston, and plundering Mughal ships and those trading with the empire. There is also the name of John Cornelius to consider as well, an alleged pirate captain who was said to have rounded Madagascar and up to the Persian Gulf with his vessel, *Morning Star*, during 1687, a few years before Raynor and his men.[3] However, the issue is that Cornelius is thought by many historians to be fictional, appearing in the second volume of compiled piratical accounts of *General History of the Pyrates*; a 1720s publication by Charles Johnson. There has been continued speculation as to whether Johnson was a pen-name utilized by Daniel DeFoe or 18th century journalist Nathaniel Mist, with many modern-day historians fairly confident in the latter. In any case, the second volume contains a few fanciful accounts of pirates that cannot be corroborated through any means of cross referencing sources. Both volumes of this work are rife with historical errors, and the author seemingly utilizing imagination to fill the gaps. This being said, whether real or fictional, Cornelius and the crew of the *Morning Star* would not exactly fit the bill of a good example of the Pirate Round, as they are said to never return. Instead the story of Cornelius and his men concludes at Madagascar following a mutiny, their ship becoming unseaworthy, and Cornelius dying upon the isle five months later.[4] Even if true, this would hardly be a successful and inspiring example to future pirates of what could be accomplished in these foreign waters.

This brings us to Thomas Tew, the most famous pirate of Rhode Island. Tew is often incorrectly credited as being the first to complete this loop aboard his ship *Amity* in 1692 as a privateer with a letter of marque issued by the governor of Bermuda, with the result being considered so staggeringly worthwhile he would repeat the process again in late 1694. The second trip of which was seemingly tempting fate, and would see him disemboweled in

(**Figure 5**: *"Henry Every," 18th century engraving*)

September by a cannonball while on deck during a conflict with a Mughal ship. While Tew did do these things, after George Raynor's successful voyage, there is an allegation that Tew had actually hit ships out of the Red Sea thrice in his career, with his well-known 1692 voyage being his second - and his first being a crewmate aboard the *Batchelor's Delight*. However, the claim is that he did so not aboard 1692's *Bachelor's Delight*, but the older ship of William Dampier and Lionel Wafer fame - but also confusingly is said to have done this in a vessel captained by either George or "Josiah" Raynor. This is an issue with the continuity of the tale of the *Bachelor's Delight*, especially since according to the claim, this same Raynor is said to return back to sea with him once more upon his 1694 trip.[5] For now, shelve the thought of Tew's relation to the current adventure of the *Bachelor's Delight*. This will make more sense once we later look into what becomes of Raynor following his voyage.

In 1695, one of the most famous pirates of all time attempted his own trial of the Pirate Round, after the success of both Raynor and Tew's respective efforts. This man was Captain Henry Every of the

*Fancy*. Much has been written of Every, and with good reason - for his exploits at sea he is remembered by many as "the Pirate King," or the "Arch Pirate." His successful raids at the Red Sea saw him accumulate riches beyond his wildest dreams and resulted with his men scattering across the Americas and back home to England while a global manhunt sought them out. Never captured, and having gotten away with his crimes, Every is considered to be one of the most successful pirates in history. Like Captain Raynor before him, he did so by assaulting vessels of the Mughal Empire.

## THE MUGHAL EMPIRE

Before proceeding with George Raynor, it is also helpful to provide a brief analysis on his targets, and why so many pirates after him rushed across the world to follow his example. Stretching from the tip of Cape Comorin in India, to modern-day Bangladesh, Assam, and northern Afghanistan, the Mughal Empire ruled the Indian subcontinent, first established in the years around 1526.[6] This emperor-led nation rose from modern-day Uzbekistan, and quickly rose and grew through military warfare, encompassing the cultures and exports as they were acquired through combat, rather than suppressing them or enforcing a replacement culture. The end result was major economic expansion, with a wide variety of exports, stretching from Persian to Indian goods, and constant imports from Africa, Arabia, and Asian wares from across the Bay of Bengal. At the time of Raynor's arrival, the current emperor was Muhi al-Din Muhammad, or more commonly referred to as Emperor "Aurangzeb," the sixth ruler of the Mughal Empire who had ruled since 1658, and would continue to do so until his later death in the year 1707. While in our current day we largely associate India's religious relations with Hinduism, in the 1690s Aurangzeb observed Islam, memorizing the Quran,[7] which projects a largely different idea of the religious goods and their appearances that were shipped out of India then as opposed to now. Yet perhaps of most importance to their maritime trade was the booming industry of textile production by Mughal artisans during the rule of Aurangzeb.

In a written account by Francois Benier, a French physician of the Mughal emperor, he detailed the quality of the textiles within their country and being shipped out of India, which were crafted masterfully by embroiders, and stating how:

*"Artisans manufacture of silk, fine brocade, and other fine muslins, of which are made turbans, robes of gold flowers, and tunics worn by females, so delicately fine as to wear out in one night, and cost even more if they were well embroidered with fine needlework.*[8]*"*

(Figure 6: Cropped portion of "Aurangzeb, Grand Moghol," by Nicolas de Larmessin, 1690)

Benier further elaborates on other practices employed, such as those originating from Persia, in which fabric became painted or block-printed, and of Pashmina shawls which would in time make their way to the European nations of England and France, as well as the orient, and had long-been adored within the empire as far back as their first emperor, Akbar.[9] Other noteable textile exports consisted of cotton calicoes, as well as fabric dyes such as indigo.

In addition to these fine textiles occupying the holds of the nation's ships abound in the Indian Ocean, there were also vast amounts of exotic spices such as pepper, cloves, and cardamom. There were also legendary riches - both raw and worked gold, silver, and mined gemstones; diamonds, emeralds, and rubies, of which jewelers utilized to create unrivaled exquisite jewelry. These goods made their way around the world not only in their own vessels, but reached further shores through the implementation of England's East India Company as far back as the turn of the 17th century. These goods making their way out of the Mughal Empire, combined with other middle-eastern cargo out of the Red Sea, such as that of the Ottoman Empire, was considered a significant turning point in the overall history of international commerce. While Dutch traders primarily focused on the exquisite textiles, the Portuguese instead turned their main attention to the spice trade.

## Rise of the Bachelor's Delight

Meanwhile, England and France both took in an interest in most all goods the Mughals were willing to export, with the two countries often vying for dominance of the maritime trade. This interest led to a massive increase of wealth to the Mughal Empire. In response to demands, the Empire doubled down on textile production as it became craved in Europe, and in return, the Mughals amassed countless fortunes.[10] The English had first interacted with the empire hoping to conduct trade as usual, only to learn that the foreigners had no need for their English goods - The Mughal Empire was self-sufficient, and most any goods England had to offer, they already possessed, or had easy access to. Other proposed imports to them couldn't be sustained, or were impractical in their warm climates. To conduct trade for the many items desired from them, European nations generally were forced to pay cash for most all things; precious silver, the established primary currency of the empire, often smelted down and re-minted into Mughal rupee coins.[11] As stated by John Ogilby, a Scottish geographer and publisher, in his 1673 work *Asia, the First Part, Being an Accurate Description of Persia, the Vast Empire of the Great Mogol, and Other Parts of India, etc.,* the empire buys all of the gold and silver upon the arrival of European ships, and that:

*"All the Gold and Silver, both coin'd and uncoin'd, which is brought thither out of other Counterys, is melted and Coin'd into Money, stamp'd with Persian characters, expressing the Name and Dignity of the King."*

Many port settlements often became bustling epicenters of maritime trade, such as Calicut and Surat: famed as one of the most gleaming and wealthy cities of their nation.[12]

But very important to the exploits of George Raynor is the Mughal Empire's connection to the Red Sea. A primary route of sea trade saw vessels leaving the port of Surat and reaching the Arabian peninsula and establishing trade with East Africa by sailing into the Gulf of Aden, through the Mandeb Strait, and then into the Red Sea. With this route, Mughals sustained trade with the Ottoman Empire, stengthening their diplomatic relations with them, and facilitating hajj pilgrimages to the city of Mecca. While the Ottoman and Mughal empires were generally

(**Figure 7**: *"Silver Rupee of Aurangzeb," private collection, 17th century*)

on good terms, a persistent point of contention between the two was the control of Persia - yet relations remained respective enough of the other to maintain maritime trade and shared religious beliefs. These all of course varied depending on the era you wish to analyze of these empires, but generally the Ottomans were at odds with European forces, assisting in anti-Catholic activities. In the year 1691, as our crew of pirates enter the Gulf of Aden, the Ottoman Empire was currently waging war, and would continue to do so until 1699, fighting against Russia, The Holy Roman Empire, and others who had banded together as the Holy League.[13]

As for maritime trade going into and out of the Red Sea at the time, it would be criminal to omit mention of Abdul Ghafur, unquestioned as the "richest merchant of his time," which earned him the title of 'Umdat-ut Tujjar' - Chief of Merchants. As of the 1690s, Ghafur is noteworthy as being the "biggest shipowner of his time" as well, owning an entire fleet of merchant vessels numbering anywhere between twenty to claims as high as fifty. He had attained considerable wealth, with which he gained further great influence on oversea commerce, and by the end of his life he left behind an inheritance equivalent of 8.5 million rupees.[14] While there is no great conversion between rupees and the US mint, which later began in 1792, based on the grams and purity percentage of their standard silver rupee when compared to the impact of a US dollar (which of course is based upon Spanish pesos), a single rupee was worth roughly 0.46 USD.[15] Still, the value of a rupee also depended on their economy, and the purchasing power to them within their country. The salary of upper-middle class Mughals were often a single rupee, with which they could reasonably buy monthly provisions and support their family. To this day the word "Mogol" still exists and is used commonly, long after the eventual fall of the Mughal Empire, the very word now indicating an individual of exponential wealth and power. Simply put, amassing the equivalent of nearly 4 million current USD during the end of the 17th century in India was astronomical. It was within the Gulf of Aden that George Raynor and his men aboard the *Bachelor's Delight* would spot and plunder one of Ghafur's ships.

## A CAPTURE OF A LIFETIME

In September the pirate crew of George Raynor sailed into the Gulf of Aden, a massive deepwater inlet of ocean-water bordered by Somalian states and the country of Yemen on the Arabian Peninsula. This inlet, during the end of the 17th century, was the sole way into and out of the Red Sea, converging down to a narrow chokepoint entrance known as the Bab-el Mandeb Strait, or by many sailors "the Babs." Other nicknames for this entrance include the Gate of Lamentation, the Gate of Grief, or the Gate of Tears.[16] These nicknames exist for good reason. To state that the Red Sea beyond is massive is an understatement, with the body of water measuring at 1,200 miles in length, and 190 miles in width at its widest. In fact, the Gulf of Aden is technically a further extension and part of the Red Sea, with the strait's formation owed to fluctuation of sea levels, which led to the definition of this portion as the gulf. Now within, beyond the Bab-el Mandeb Strait, this sea's coastline is understandably dotted with many coastal port settlements and cities, all of whom conduct maritime trade with each other, but are isolated from the rest of the world otherwise regarding the waters. This results in countless ships constantly and reliably being funneled through a single entrance and exit - and this is where pirates sat awaiting prey. Exports leaving the Red Sea, and imports from all over the world would see ships venturing into the straight, never knowing what awaited them on the opposite side. Ships confronted with pirates could simply be cutoff and their path reasonably blocked with threats of conflict, and efforts to flee into the Red Sea was akin to backing one's self into a corner, and fleeing into the gulf and then southward usually risked the ire of pirates as well.

Nowadays this particular issue has long-been remedied with the construction of the Suez Canal by the French in the 1850s and 1860s, which saw much effort connecting the Red Sea to the Mediterranean Sea for vessels, and opening the possibility of new routes to the Indian Ocean and beyond without every single ship out of Europe having to encircle the entire African continent first and deal with pirates operating out of Madagascar. In fact, during a recent maritime crisis in the year 2021, the ultra-large G-class container ship, *Ever Given*, became lodged in the Suez Canal, running aground and rotating sideways - completely blocking it in both directions.[17] Until the obstruction was cleared, six days later, it set shipping routes firmly back to the early 19th century and prior, like the days of George Raynor. The impact that the incident had on maritime trade was felt globally, with international shipping having to round the Cape of Good Hope as they had in olden days, and there were immediate concerns of piracy out of Somalia.

While Raynor and his crew had opted to travel this far from their familiar home port of Jamaica, it is unknown what had been their true motives or goals. Piratical endeavors to the Red Sea and back, again the "Pirate Round," had not yet become popularized - unknown to them, they were pioneering it. Perhaps the end goal was to have left the West Indies for good, for a lifetime of piracy surrounding India. Even operating out of Madagascar had yet to become popularized with a pirate haven; coincidentally enough, the crew of the *Bachelor's Delight* would go on to become the first to partake in what the island offered in the form of a haven, sponsored by criminal Adam Baldridge. The pirates had opted to not pause at Madagascar on their way along the African shores, and instead sailed straight for the Red Sea, and while they could have assaulted any number of merchant vessels, they happened upon one belonging to Abdul Ghafur. One of, if not their first, attempts upon arrival to the Gulf of Aden. There is however the possiblity that they may have first robbed a Portuguese vessel or two, and feeling unfulfilled, pressed on until hitting the ship owned by Ghafur.

(**Figure 8**: *"Attacking the Ship from India," Unknown artist, 1837*)

While the assault occurred during early September, the primary period account of the act of piracy is found within the *Diary and Consultation Book of 1691 of Fort St. George*; Fort St. George being an English-established fortress in India for the East India Company. The report relays the news of their piracy reaching Fort St. George:

*"Receiving yesterday overland advices from Surrat of the 13th September last, wherein they give us the Sad newes of their reconfinement by reason a Moors Ship from Mocha was taken by an European Pyrat, the Merchants reporting her to be a Companys Ship & therefore required Satisfaction, Whereupon the Agent &" were confind under gaurd & applyd by letters to the King & to be freed from their gaurds and aspersions, and their Shipps from the embargoes they were under.[18]"*

A later report in the same publication, dated in December re-touches on the assault in the context of being concerned of the safety of vessels as of recent, again pointing to the acts of the *Bachelor's Delight*:

*"...it was reported that a Surrat Moorship comeing from Mocho with a rich Cargoe to the Vallue of 900000 rupees was Seized and taken by an English Shipp affirming to belong to ye Honorable Company, whereupon ye Agent &c were sent for, to discourse them about it, wich they endeavour'd to Satisfye the Goverment in, by Saying that this Action might possibly be committed by Some Pyratts under English Coulors, or their Enimyes the Danes..."*

To paraphrase, the pirates had engaged and captured a Mughal merchant ship prior to September 13th. She had been loaded with rich cargo, worth an estimated 900,000 rupees, or thereabouts. These reports of course do not mention Raynor nor the *Bachelor's Delight* by name, but even the assaulted crew had difficulty coming to a conclusive answer to what nation the violent ship belonged to. However, this account corroborates the dates and numbers recorded by Adam Baldridge on Madagascar where Raynor and crew would next head after the successful plunder of such a wealthy Mughal ship, not falling victim to greed and pressing their luck even further. A total of 900,000 rupees worth of treasure and cargo is no small amount, it was enough to set the pirates for the remainder of their lives, and was an amount potentially felt by Abdul Ghafur. Yet those numbers, fortunately for the crew of the *Bachelor's Delight*, did not cause an outrage from Emperor Aurangzeb, unlike Henry Every's capture of the *Ganj-i-Sawai* of the Grand Mughal Fleet in 1695, which resulted in a global manhunt with Every forced to go into hiding, and his crew scattering across the globe and one by one snatched up by authorities. The crew of Captain Raynor had admittedly hit the sweet spot - enough treasure to live comfortably for the rest of their lives, but did so without invoking the ire of all nations.

The aforementioned reports of the assault are not alone, with others relaying additional pieces of the puzzle, the next being records within the 1696 book *A Voyage to Surratt in the Year 1689 Giving a Large Account of That City and It's Inhabitants and of the English Factory There*, by John Ovington. It more accurately clarifies a date, August 27th, or immediately before; which is indeed prior to September 13th, stating:

*"...that a Rich Moor-ship belonging to one Abdel Gheford, was taken by Hat-men, that is, in their Dialect, Europeans; and therefore 'till Restitution is made by them of nine Lacks of Roupies, which exceeds the value of 100,000 Sterling, no liberty must be granted. The Ship was in her Passage from Mocha to Surratt, and tho' the Indians were averse to from Fighting, or hazarding their lives for four Roupies a Month...*[19]*"*

And lastly, a third report brings to light more conclusions and some of the action bits omitted from the previous accounts. This following account comes from the director of the East India Company in Surat:

*"...the ship more was attacked, there were several Turks above who made a vigorous defense, but after having had twelve men killed and around twenty wounded, it was necessary yield to force. The corsairs took control of the ship from which they removed 450,000 pieces of eight [in value], they found there maneuvers and other things that accomodated them and some of the best of the crew to serve on board and left the rest with this vessel.*[20]*"*

It also goes on to state that the assurement of the pirates being English led to much rioting and assembled efforts in the streets to pillage the lodge of the East India Company in outrage. The act performed by the English pirates also halted three English Company vessels from being permitted to leave, on account of suspicion until approved by the Great Mogol [Aurangzeb]. It is unfortunate, however, that the Mughal ship had not been recorded by name by either the Fort St. George accounts, or those made by Baldridge after their arrival to Madagascar following this event.

In synopsis, gleaned from the reports, these English pirates assaulted a Mughal ship belonging to Abdul Ghafur on or around August 27th, 1691, that had been traveling from the port of Mocha in the Red Sea bound for Surat, and crewed at least partially by Turks. The vessel had been laden with rich wares and treasure likely in excess of 100,000 rupees worth, or about 450,000 pieces of eight equivalent. This treasure likely consisted of a variety valuable coins, jewelry, artwork, textiles, and surely some coffee - a major export out of Mocha. The capture was no simple surrender; caving in to the pirates' demands was preceeded by much bloodshed resulting in twelve of the Mughal crew being killed, and another twenty having been wounded in some way. After the riches of the vessel had been plundered and relocated to the *Bachelor's Delight*, they allowed the ship and her surviving crew to limp on to Surat; but not without pressganging, that is to force, some of her most useful crew into joining Raynor's men. This was a common practice amid pirates, with particularly valuable skilled sailors such as carpenters, physicians, and cooks often spared from death and forced into pirate crews.

Having made successful plunder of a massive fortune, and in theory having suffered at least something in retaliation from the Mughal vessel, Captain Raynor decreed the ship sail south, bound for the island of Madagascar to repair and resupply before another return voyage back across the Atlantic. His orders were not contested.

Yet, before we move on, there is a slight possibility that they spent a small amount of time off of Cape Comorin, India's southern-most tip, albeit unlikely. Relayed from the port of Calicut later in November by Captain Robert Knox of the East India Trade Company, commander of the *Tonkin Merchant*. Even if so, Knox states that the unspecified pirates he had encountered months prior had meant him no harm and went on their way.[21]

# CHAPTER
# Three

*The Voyage Home*

The tropical island of Madagascar resides in the Indian Ocean off the coast of southeast Africa, and is known for both its beauty and biodiversity. Seemingly small in comparison to the adjacent continent of Africa, this island is one of the largest on the planet, roughly two and half times the size of the United Kingdom, or for American context, Madagascar is roughly the same total landmass as the state of Texas; just in an elongated oblong shape. A snapshot of the island during the 17th century would see the native Malagasy natives engaging in commerce with all manner of seafaring traders and slavers, partaking in both import and export of both. Their tribes consisted of both shipwrecked sailors who had been respected for their nautical skills and who had risen through ranks amid them, while other tribes might possess enslaved Europeans. Likewise, the natives of Madagascar themselves were victimized by the transatlantic slave trade, captured and exported no differently than those of the African mainland. Further, most all European attempts to colonize or settle on the island inevitably failed, often ending in much bloodshed. The tribes would agree to trade with foreigners, yes, but often found themselves at war with one another, leading to most of the islanders being very competent in guerilla style jungle warfare - which European visitors were generally unprepared for.

(**Figure 9**: *"Map of Madagascar, 1685," by Alain Manesson Mallet. Note the slender coastal isle titled Isla Maria along the eastern coast, and Fort Dauphin to the south*)

## The Voyage Home

As mentioned previously, France did put forth a valiant effort with 1643's Fort Dauphin, or "Fort Dolphin" as pronounced by the English, located at the island's most southeastern tip. This jutting peninsula was perfectly located for settlement, and from here French sailors operated from for a good thirty year stretch before being wiped out by the native peoples, with survivors rounded up and extracted from the dangerous isle. Although this conflict occurred in 1674, by the 1690s the natives had long since opted to operate out of the French ruins, continuing commerce with sailors, offering goods and resupply for upcoming long voyages, often in exchange for coveted firearms.

Meanwhile, further north along the eastern shore of Madagascar, the criminal Adam Baldridge had arrived in July of 1690 along with a young lad named John King. Like Raynor's pirates, Baldridge too had fled the waters of Jamaica, albeit on account of murder charges. It has long-been suspected that Baldridge himself may have been a pirate before this point in his 'career,' but the claims have always been unfounded, but he likely at least had some experience as a sailor or merchant. We do know that a deposition made by a Samuel Perkins in August of 1698, when discussing matters of piracy in regard to the actions of Henry Every in the Red Sea, that Perkins described Baldridge, and that:

*"...he was informed [that Adam Baldridge] had formerly killed a man in Jamaica, and thereupon turned pirate about 13 years ago [in 1685].*[1]*"*

However, this single mention could just as likely be hearsay. Over the last year since their arrival, the two had lived on the isle peacefully with the natives, of which he offered services as a mediator between warring factions, and assisted in facilitating trade between their native tongue and the variety of languages possessed by visiting ships - some of which Baldridge was familiar. If nothing else, he understood the local Malagasy and spoke fluent English, for this alone he proved useful to them. No longer would discussions of international trade require days of effort to come to conclusions with slavers and pirates as they struggled with language barrier.

Baldridge did not setup along the mainland however, instead he'd opted for the island of St. Mary, also known as Sainte-Marie, or in modern times, Nosy Boraha. The isle had gained its name long ago in 1503 by Portuguese sailors after having survived a shipwreck, naming it in honor of the Christian Virgin Mary. Yet at the end of the 16th century, it also received the name of Nosin'Iborahimo, a Malagasy word, by the captain of a Dutch vessel which had arrived to her shores for supplies. It is worth mentioning that a local legend speaks of another reason for its name; of a native islander named Boraha, who while out fishing, was dragged away by a whale. Lost at sea, Boraha was saved by a fish named "Sorokay" which led the lad back to dry land, which he named after himself. Regardless of the origin of its name, to this very day natives have long since perpetuated the folklore, with the descendants of Boraha being deemed forbidden to eat the local Sorokay fish of the surrounding waters.[2]

It was here Baldridge would establish a pirate haven that would quickly reach unforseen heights, become known across the world, and become the basis for rumors blown out of proportion and legends. It would go on to be generally known as "the pirate haven of St. Mary's." It was with this protected haven that pirates would gain a base of operations to strike out from, return to, and attain needed European goods and supplies - which led to longer stays without as much of a timecrunch to return to the Americas. Having constructed a home overlooking the bay, which would be armed with cannons to deter those that meant ill-will to him or visiting pirates, Baldridge was essentially self-proclaimed king of this location, and willing to trade goods he would acquire from shipments originating from New York and potentially other colonies to the sailors that needed them, and in return Baldridge would receive weaponry and riches plundered by the pirates from their exploits in the Indian Ocean and Red Sea. Amid those supporting his endeavor even included Frederick Philipse, a prominent merchant out of New York whose actions were condoned and supported by their governor, Benjamin Fletcher, of whom also would go on to call pirate Thomas Tew amid his circle of friends in time.[3] Once the entrepreneur was established on the island of St. Mary, Adam Baldridge's first customers, so to speak, would arrive on the 13th of October, 1691 - George Raynor and the crew of the *Bachelor's Delight*.

# The Voyage Home

(**Figure 10**: *Cropped portion of "Sainte Marie Island - Madagascar, 1601," by Etienne de Flacourt. Baldridge would establish his pirate haven at the location of the bay toward the southern end of the island*)

Baldridge would continue operating this haven and profiting from those wishing to utilize his services up until 1697. Upon his return to New York as wealthy and successful merchant, Baldridge would provide a deposition recorded as a transcript, to Lord Bellomont, Richard Coote, governor of the Colony of New York. Within, Baldridge records his activities on St. Mary's Island all the business and transactions recording during his time there. He had built a trading enterprise that brought him from being penniless, to a wealthy businessman, and from being an obscure figure in history to one of famed notoriety. He had built a career for himself in a tropical paradise with everything he needed. It is unknown, Baldridge's reason for calling it quits and heading back across the Atlantic, but many point towards a native uprising against him after selling a number of them into slavery. Still, his final actions at the island suggested his departure had been planned anyways. In any case, when presenting his expertise as a trader, albeit a supporter of pirates, in 1699, Baldridge details the arrival of George Raynor and his crew, the first of the pirates to his isle, on October 13th of 1691, following their capture of the Mughal ship. He states their arrival in detail:

*"October 13, 1691. Arrived the Bachelor's Delight, Captain Georg Raynor Commander, Burden 180 Tons or there abouts, 14 Guns, 70 or 80 men, that had made a voyage into the Red Seas and taken a ship belonging to the Moors, as the men did report, where they took as much money as made the whole share run about 1,100 1. a man. They Careened at St. Maries, and while they Careened I supplyed them with Cattel for their present spending and they gave me for my Cattel a quantity of Beads, five great Guns for a fortification, some powder and shott, six Barrells of flower, about 70 barrs of Iron.*[4]*"*

We see here that not only had Raynor and crew been his first customer, of which they were provided great assistance, but the crew of the Bachelor's Delight provided the initial foundations for which Baldridge to get the ball rolling, so to speak, for the establishment of what would go on to be a legendary pirate haven, providing him with initial cannons with which to protect the island and its bays. He also notes the considerable wealth the crew possessed, divvied between them with each holder of a share of loot with about £1,100 each. For context, during the period an experienced sailors wage would see them earning about £25 per year of seafaring labor. These men each held literal fortunes that would set them for life. Barring the temptation of greed, these men would never once again have to resort to crime.

As for Baldridge's mention of careening, this was a commonly performed and ardous task considered vital for the wellbeing of ships. The process involved bringing the vessel alongside a suitable stretch of beach and unloading most of her cargo to shore, often inlcuding a few cannon which the sailors would position aimed out to sea in the case the operation needed to be defended. Then, the vessel would slowly be tilted to her side and hauled up ashore, exposing half of her hull normally concealed beneath the water line. It was here that all manners of issues would plague ships after time at sea. Barnacles would attach themselves to the hull, which in turn provided a course and jagged surface for which seaweed and other vegetal detritus to become attached. While so far not seemingly harmful, this impacted the drag of the ship, and affected her speed in the water. Speed was very important for many reasons, but for the vehicle of seafaring criminals, a cleaned hull or not may be the single factor that resulted in the success or failure of chasing down a prey ship, or whether the pirates could escape pursuit by authorities when outgunned or outmanned. Futher, teredo worms were notoriously drawn to shipwood, burrowing themselves into the hulls of ships. As one can imagine, holes in the hull of a ship is a very bad thing. These sea critters had to be extracted, and their holes plugged with whatever was available, usually a mixture of things slathered in tar. Once the process was complete, which again was no easy task, it was time to re-orient the ship and expose her other side - and do it all again. Keep in mind, this entire time the pirates are essentially sitting ducks if happened upon. Sure, they could attempt to defend the beach with their guns, but if overpowered their only option would be to abandon their ship, their cargo, their acquired loot and flee inland; and on an island, there's limited places to run. This is where pirate havens came into play, offering security, additional numbers and potentially ships around on your side, and the haven itself bolstering the defenses of the area with cannon of their own to repel attackers.

It was for these purposes, pirates often appreciated the idea of a haven, even if it meant a fee, or putting their differences aside with a rival. As for careening, it was not only a laborious task, but a lengthy

(**Figure 11**: *Period depiction of pirates careening their vessel in a tropical setting*)

one. As Baldridge states, George Raynor and his men would remain at the haven of St. Mary's until the 4th of November, 1691, having spent twenty-two days at St. Mary's. This is also a good time to analyze Baldridge's description of the *Bachelor's Delight*, which up until this point has only briefly been decribed as the re-named French ship *La Constance* out of Rochelle, France. To surmise the type of vessel we have been imagining thus far, the described statistics are very close to the *Queen Anne's Revenge* of later Blackbeard fame, which had previously been the French frigate, *La Concorde*. It had been a 200-ton ship, armed with 16 cannon, and crewed by about 75 men. While this is not definitive proof that *Constance/Loyal Jamaica/Bachelor's Delight* had been a French frigate, the comparisons are very close, only slightly smaller. Raynor's crew of 70-80 men as opposed to *Queen Anne's Revenge*'s 75, and 14 cannon as opposed to 16, with the ship being burthen 180 tons as compared to the 200 of *Queen Anne's Revenge*. For now, we will assume she is a French frigate, but keep in mind that there is a the possiblity she could instead is a ketch or pink. These would be impressive numbers for a smaller ship, but keep in mind that Blackbeard overloaded ships beyond the number of men they were designed to be operated by. Ketches and Sloops not being too dissimilar, the vessels were designed to be ran by about ten individuals - and Blackbeard crammed 120 onto one. So, crew numbers are hard to justify.

Now, the entire time spent on the island was surely not entirely non-stop repair, but also a reprieve from their long time out at sea, and certainly included leisurely activities as well. This could measure anywhere between lounging and conversing with King, Baldridge, and

## The Voyage Home

Baldridge's alleged native wife, whom he had essentially married to cement himself amid the Malagasy people and their land, to perhaps fishing or hunting wildlife. The waters immediately around the island offered good variety of barracuda, bonita, jackfish, tuna, and the deeper waters harbored dolpins, manta rays and reef sharks. For those who spent time away from the careening work and opted to trek inland, they would have trudged through tropical rainforest undergrowth and bore witness to a number of amphibians and gecko amid the forest and water-logged mangrove trees. Without at doubt, at least one of the pirates had to have seen a lemur; three species of which populate St. Mary's, including the admittedly adorable and wide-eyed "fat-tailed dwarf lemur.[5]" This time spent on the tropical Madagascar surely was a memory that remained in the crew's minds for the rest of their lives.

Now, as Baldridge recalls this experience in the past tense, from the year 1699, he also recounts having heard word of their end result following their departure from his establishment. After stopping by Port Dolphin (Fort Dauphin) on Madagascar to take in provision, that they later set sail on the 9th of December they set sail bound for America, where:

*"I have heard since they arrived to Carolina and Complyed with the owners, giveing them for Ruin of the Ship three thousand pounds, as I have heard since.[6]"*

Arriving down to Fort Dauphin, a more arid region of Madagascar, the crew likely knew via Baldridge what they were getting into; that it no longer was it a settlement controlled by the French, but the natives. While Baldridge operated the pirate haven, offering protection and goods, Dauphin had been an established coastal trading stop for nearly fifty years, even following the exodus of the French and occupation of the natives. It is apparent simply from the crew's need to resupply here that Baldridge was, at least early into the time of the haven, unable to provide all they needed for a return trip to the Americas. The natives of Fort Dauphin were accustomed to interacting with traders of a variety of nations, and apparently a few things had to be worked out and plans established before departing, as the pirates spent just over four weeks there before finally setting sail in December back towards the Atlantic.

Its likely many things discussed in Madagascar amid the crew pertained to where the *Bachelor's Delight* would next sail, and a course of action decided upon based on their accrued plundered wealth.

The other thing to consider here is who opted to even return to the west. Madagascar acted as an ending to many sailors' careers, from shipwrecked sailors who had no alternatives, to pirates opting to integrate themselves into the native societies for the remainder of their lives. If author Charles Johnson is to be believed, within his *General History of the Pyrates*, some of these even went on to become "princes" amid the Malagasy people, enjoying respect for their skills and partaking in the peoples' views on polygamy. This is particularly questioned, regarding a variety of conflicting reports of the men who would later arrive to Carolina after this point. One might note that Baldridge states the pirates arrived with a crew of 70 to 80 men. Also note that the reports from Surat also state the crew having pressed a number of skilled Turkish sailors into their crew against their will. When these pirates later arrive to Carolina's shores, a collection of numbers are cited, stating they arrive as a crew of 26 to 80 - but bear no mention of any middle eastern crewmembers. Other accounts state closer to 40 for her crew, which would certainly indicate that some of their number was left behind either here at Madagascar, or at one of their remaining two stops en-route. An often-cited number is 26, the names of which many are easily discoverable in Charleston records. If this lowest number is the case, the *Bachelor's Delight* certainly left crew behind who did not agree with the decision to sail for Carolina. This works both ways as well. Of the 26 or more crew that eventually arrive to Carolina, historians are unsure how many of them had actually been participants of the ship's piratical endeavors in the Red Sea, aside from the general claim of the crew arriving with shares of the plunder. The two subsequent stops from here leave limited opportunities for others to join her crew before arriving to Carolina, but that isn't to say that individuals couldn't have been picked up in either Baldridge's haven of St. Mary's, or here at Fort Dauphin.

There are certainly some who may have lobbied for the destination of the *Bachelor's Delight*, such as crewmated Daniel Horry and Francis Blanchard, who already had families living in Carolina, and those

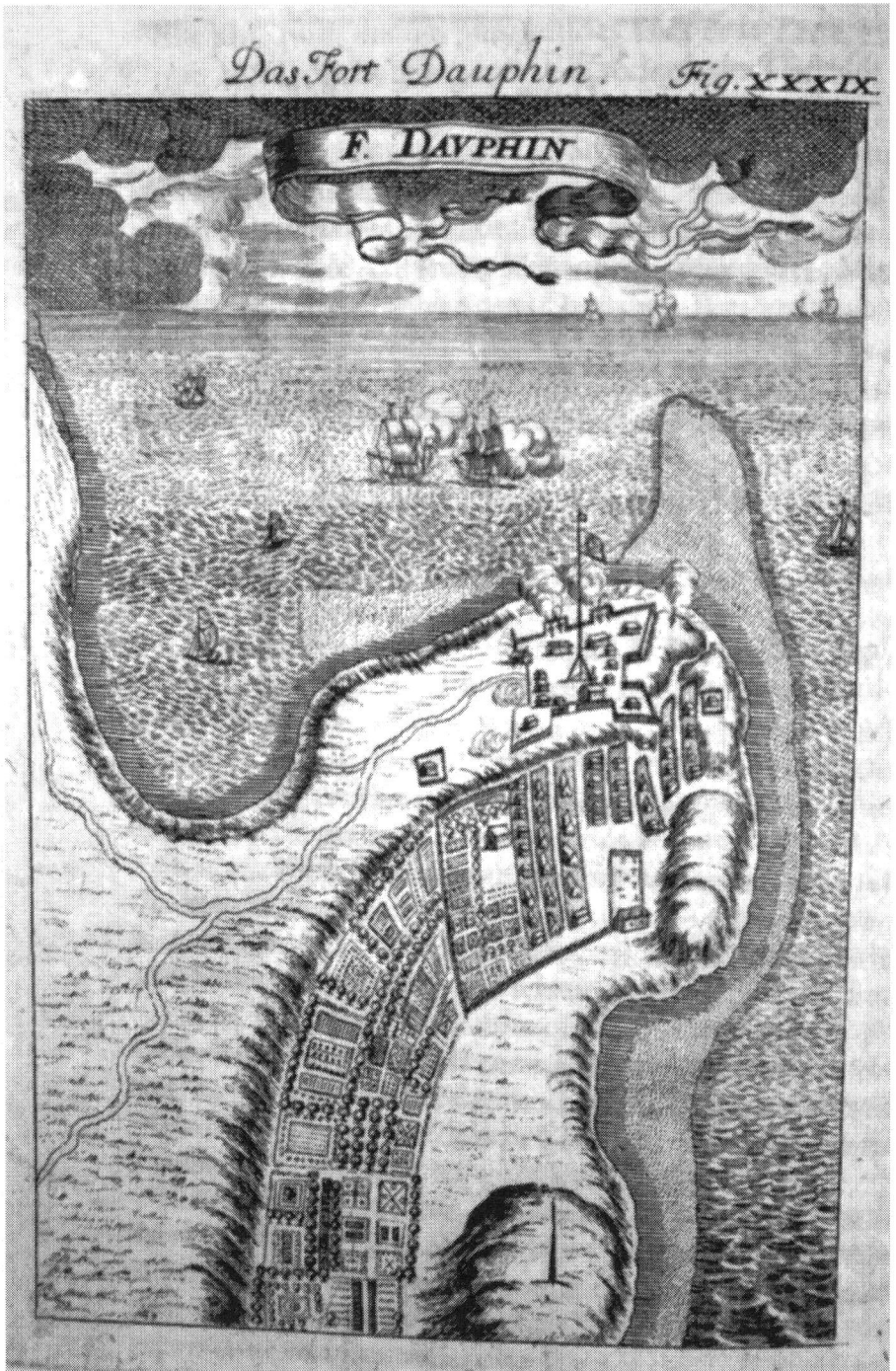

(**Figure 12**: *"View of Fort Dauphin (Madagascar), 1685," by Alain Manesson Mallet*)

familiar with politics would know that governor Seth Sothel currently ruled over Charles Towne in southern Carolina, or at least had been upon their departure from Jamaica.[7]

Sothel had been known for his history of fraudulent crimes as governor of North Carolina and antics prior, and faced trial which saw him exiled and banned from being part of any office of North Carolina during 1689. He would venture down to South Carolina and proclaimed himself governor in 1690 when Raynor was but a crewmate of the *Mary*. Sothel was exactly the type of governor the pirates would hope to interact with, arriving from across the world with foreign treasures, yet still clutching a commision issued for the *Loyal Jamaica* to legally go on the account. Sothel would certainly be the type to look the other way regarding the name of Harrison on the commission and likely allow them free reign to do as they please.[8]

For now, we'll assume that some number of the crew opted to remain behind here on Madagascar, and the crew pressed on to South Carolina's port of Charles Towne, in their same vessel, *Bachelor's Delight*, previously known as the *Loyal Jamaica*, previously known as *Constance*. While there is speculation that crew would next be interested in sailing for the West Indies before Carolina, their next stop would be at Ascension Island in the Atlantic.

On the 9th of January, a full month after departing Fort Dauphin, the *Bachelor's Delight* would spot the uninhabited volcanic Ascension Island on the horizon. It was here along the isle's yellow sandy shores that they would spot a pair of Danish shipwrecked sailors and come to their aid. The men had been Peter Skroder and Cent Direckson, who upon spotting the sails of their vessel had affixed their ragged white shirts to sticks as makeshift flags in attempts to signal need of aid to the passing ship. According to the later *Deposition of Peter Skroder*, a Danish male aged twenty-four years, and who arrived to Charles Towne months later as a member of the crew:

## The Voyage Home

*"Last he the said Deponent in Company with: Cent Direckson did See a Saile of the Island of assencion on which they made a signe[l] with: two white Shirts upon which the vesell came nere who had alsoe business there as they understood to turn turtle for Provisions & they Desired the Ship to take them one board and Carry & put them one Shoare and they answereds it was a Christian worke and they would doe it & would either Putt them one Some Christian Shoare or one bard Some Christian Ship.⁹"*

Peter would go on to state that the crew of the pirates would linger about Ascension Island for a total of about twenty-four hours before departing. This island was very remote, located in the middle of the Atlantic nearly perfectly between Brazil and Africa, and was a terrible place for a sailor to end up, as there are virtually no sources of fresh water aside from where moisture seeps through rocks on ithe isle's upper slopes, rainfall was typically consistent during only March through May, and generally the lowlands were generally therefore arid and desert-like.¹⁰ Later in 1701, upon the arrival of William Dampier aboard HMS *Roebuck*, a minor freshwater source was eventually later named for him for his discovery while marooned for weeks, dubbed "Dampier's Drip," located in Breakneck Valley.¹¹ The crew of the *Bachelor's Delight* had not arrived to the isle in search of water however, instead they had come to Ascension to harvest sea turtles for meat, a fairly common practice often referred to as "turtling."

As for their next interaction along the seas upon their departure from Ascension Island with the Danes aboard, this information too was provided by the rescued Skroder.

*"In the Lattitude of Surranam they mett with a vessell under Dutch Collours mounted with Six Guns or thereabouts where they willingly would have spoken with to have putt the deponent [Peter Skroder] one board [aboard] of the Ship and to have Gotten Some Reliefe of Lyquors & Provisions from them.¹²"*

However, the Dutch vessel would not want to risk the interaction with this strange vessel, and instead, as Peter describes, instead opted to discharge her guns and put a cannonball through the sails of the

(**Figure 13**: *"Fernando de Noronha," photography by Cassinha Magalhaes*)

*Bachelor's Delight*. It was not but shortly afterwards after that the crew had generally agreed that the route for Carolina was best, where they could use their plundered wealth to settle as planters of the colony and purchase plantations. He would also note the next stop of the vessel would be upon the shores of an *"Island Called ffarrdinando to water."* This was the island of Fernando de Noronha, which they then voyaged to and ventured ashore with the purpose of restocking fresh water on board their ship.[13]

Fernando de Noronha was part of an archipelago off the northeastern tip of Brazil. Admittedly a little bit out of the way while en-route to the shores of Carolina, but Ascension Island's lack of readily accessible water sources saw them making this brief detour. While the island had been used long before, by the Portuguese as a source of trade with natives for precious brazilwood, a valuable natural red dye, the isle was otherwise uninhabited and was a suitable location for the pirates to collect freshwater much easier than on Ascension Island. They would also not be the only pirates to ever visit here either, as the isle would later be visited by famous pirate Captain Bartholomew Roberts as well during the 1720s.

## *The Voyage Home*

From here the pirates would press onward, making no further stops, and instead headed straight for the southern Carolina, to the port of Charles Towne. Weaving past the Caribbean isles, and making no stop at Bermuda, the southeastern shores of North America rested upon their horizon. A decision was made to rename the vessel back to the *Loyal Jamaica* once more, fitting the name once more upon their legally issued privateering commission, the rules of which they had since of course broken in many ways. Renamed, and with her crew in aggreeance, the tentative decision was made to approach the English port, ready to present their tale of adventure as 'legal privateers' to the governor, Seth Sothel.

## Arabian Gold: Charleston's Red Sea Pirates of 1692

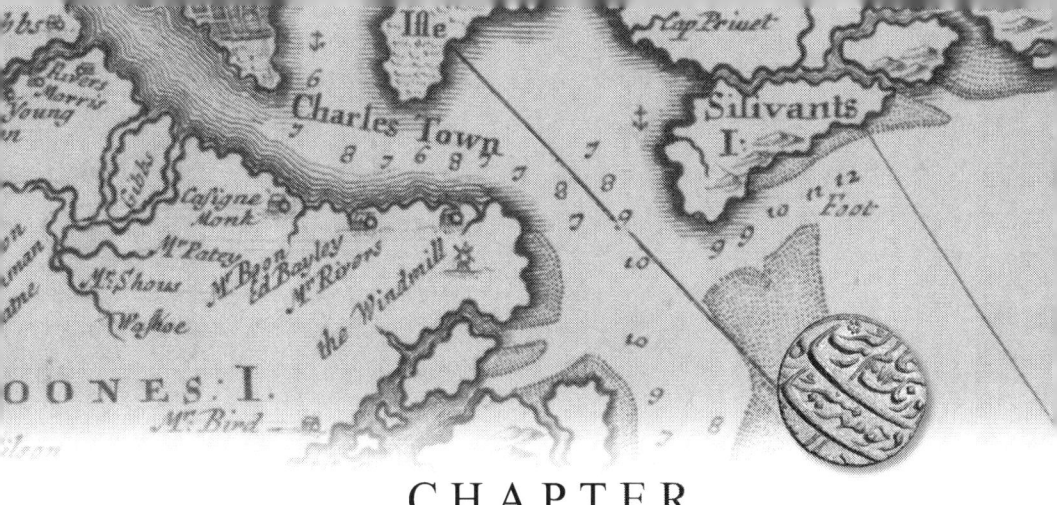

CHAPTER
# Four

### *Charles Towne, South Carolina*

To their dismay, Seth Sothel was no longer the governor. This fact would be discovered by the men of the *Loyal Jamaica* only once they had arrived to Carolina. This was a potential problem for the crew. Rather than fully enter the harbor and dock, they opted to instead sit out at the location of 'Rebellion Road' - a particular spot in the harbor just outside of the port's cannon range. This time was about mid-April of 1692, and for several days their ship sat mysteriously and ominously. It is believed that in some way or form, Raynor and his men came into the knowledge that the corrupt Seth Sothel no longer ran the English colony, and was instead a new 'by-the-books' individual named Ludwell who now acted as governor. This information likely stemmed from their brief interaction with a vessel along the coast named *Richard and Mary*, under the command of a Captain Daniel Bradley.[1] This contact may have also been the one to have informed the people of Charles Towne the name of Raynor, as without having made contact with the pirates, and without Raynor having sent any men ashore, a letter was addressed and delivered to him, calling him by name. The letter reads:

"To Capt. George Rainer Comander of the Ship now Rideing within Sullivans Island...Whereas you have for Severall dayes been at anchor with your Ship while in this port & have not Entered your said Ship in theire Majesties officies according to Law & ye times being Dangerous & troublesome: These are therefore to Require you to Imediately to Enter your said Shipp according to Law or else to Depart this Porth within forty Eight houres wind and weather permissing or the first faire wind after as you shall answere the Contrary at your will. Dated 13th. April: 1692.[2]"

The pirates sat at anchor for the following two days, they then, without a word, departed. During this time, word had been issued to inhabitants of the town to not approach the mysterious ship, and that strict and secure watch must be kept every night.[3] Obviously still weighing their options without Sothel to reliably grant them forgiveness, they milled about the Carolina coast for days, and were suspected by the Council of Charles Towne to have been gone for good, until on the 19th it was reported that their ship had been spotted, now at anchor behind Sullivan's Island, a nearby barrier isle.

Plans had been made to send several ship masters out to investigate the vessel, but on the 20th, the two Danish sailors the pirates had picked up at Ascension Island, Peter and Cent, were designated as crew to be sent into the town. Upon which, they were questioned heavily, under much scrutiny by governor Ludwell. These interactions were recorded as the *Deposition of Peter Skroder*, where much of the information regarding the crews' actions since Madagascar originate. Peter is recorded as saying on behalf of the crew that:

"...they kept very good order with Dayly Prayers peacable behavioure & that they did often Discourse & aver that they nevere had done wrong to any Christian Nation...[4]"

Skroder said little else, and certainly did not disclose the actions of the ship or her crew at Madagascar or prior. Three more days would pass before news was reported again about the mysterious ship, this time being noted on the 23rd of April that information had been reported to the Council that the ship was found abandoned, floating at anchor near

# Charles Towne, South Carolina

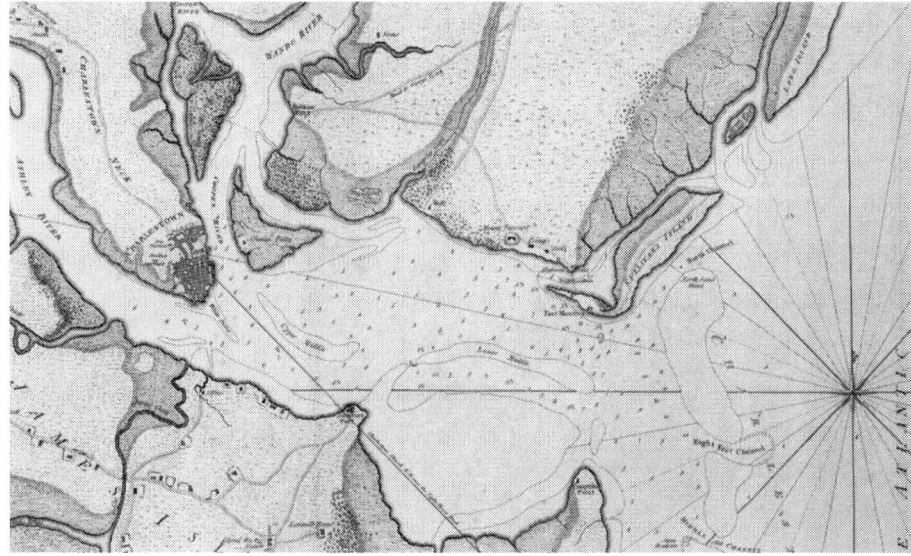

(**Figure 14**: *Cropped portion of "A Plan of the Town, Bar, Harbour and environs, of Charlestown in South Carolina..., 1780," by William Faden*)

the Hunting Islands, known by us in modern times as the slender Isle of Palms and nearby Dewees Island. The ship was reportedly:

"*...pillaged of all the Goods that was on board her & all the valluable Rigging and Sailes & of a great quantaty of money and Divers* [diverse] *other Riches.*"

This raised concerns by governor Philip Ludwell and the Council, leading them to suspect that the sailors of this ship were actually pirates, and an order was established that members of the Council, and all other Justices of the peace and constables to put forth as much effort as possible to seize any of the aforementioned goods, money, rigging, and to apprehend the suspected pirates.

By the 6th of May, it had been discovered that the ship's position was slightly incorrect, and that she had instead been anchored in Seewee Bay adjacent to Bull Island. Note that this refers to modern day Bull's Bay, and not modern-day Seewee Bay, which eventually was a name bestowed to a smaller body of water amid the marsh between the isle and the mainland. The ship had finally taken on a name as well, the

(**Figure 15**: *"Portrait believed to depict governor Philip Ludwell"*)

people of Charles Towne referring to her simply as "the privateer." Now, this isn't quite as black and white of a term as it actually legally was, the terms pirate and privateer were used rather interchangably during the period. It was a fine line, they were weaponized private sailors that may or may not have had a piece of paper. By this point, no one in town was familiar with the ship's name, let alone the specifics of how these men operated or what they had done. Still, by the 6th, her crew had already made their way into Charles Town under the radar, so to speak. This news saw a proclamation to the citizens of the port town in the afternoon, forbidding them to harbor or conceal these unknown men in their homes, and encouraged turning them in or providing information on their whereabouts so they could be captured.[5]

The following afternoon, the Council would gather once more as one of the crew of the ship approached willing to speak. His name was Richard Abram, and he confessed to being a member of her crew, at least long enough to have seen her plunder several vessels. It was ordered that it be illegal for Richard Abram to depart Charles Towne by land or sea for an entire year. A few days later, the ship, noted as being a destitute wreck, was brought into the town's harbor on the 11th. On the 14th, it was decreed that Captain George Raynor and the rest of his company that had come ashore, now commonly known as "the privateers," are lawfully required to present themselves on or by the 26th, and upon the 26th they would be subject to being examined and attest their intent and present their confessions. Further, these men were forbade by law their departure from the Province of Carolina during the next twelve months.[6]

Before the month of May drew to a close, presumably between the 14th and the 26th, Captain George Raynor did come forth to the Council, along with twenty-one of his crew who agreed to do so. While there is mysteriously no recorded transcript of their initial depositions, the cases they made for themselves, or what claims they presented about their time at sea, it was certainly wrapped up quietly between the wealthy pirates and the town officials; who gave no indication going forward believing them to be pirates, but as having had arrived simply as innocent legal privateers. Located in the appendix of the *Journal of the Grand Council of Carolina April 11, 1692-September 26, 1692*, a work edited and compiled in 1907 by Alexander S. Salley Jr., the Secretary of the Historical Commission of South Carolina, is primarily from where this information is presented. In which it declares that:

*"The under named persons arraived in this part of the Province, the* [blank] *day of Aprill Anno : Domi 1692, in the shipp Called, the Loyall Jamaica : Commonly called the Privateer vessel, each man entered into Recognizance with Securitys in the Moneth of May, 1692, In the Sumes, to their Names annexed for one yeare, or until the Government, Heard from England -"*

It then goes on to present the names of the crew who came forth. I will opt to present them alphabetically by first name in bold. The two names that follow each are their securities - essentially Charles Towne citizens that vouch for the crewmember's good name and integrity, willing to put their own finances and good name on the line so to speak. Listed after each crewmember's name is the amount that they paid in pounds for their own bail. If any of these men were to leave the Province within a year, the two individuals who acted as their securities would each pay to the government the amount of pounds listed after their names.

**Adam Richardson** (£50) - Robert Gibbs, William Bradley (£25)
**Christopher Linckley** (£40) - Charles Basden, William Smith (£20)
**Daniel Hory** (£50) - Isaac Massique, Peter Girrard (£25)
**Daniel Rawlinson** (£60) - Nicholas Marden, Francis Fidling (30)
**Edmund Medlicotte** (£80) - Charles Basden, Peter Girrard (£20)
**Francis Blanchard** (£40) - Peter LaSall, John Thomas (£20)
**George Raynor** (£400) - John Alexander, William Smith (£200)
**James Gillchriste** (£100) - John Alexander, Andrew Baugh (£50)
**John Palmer** (£40) - Joseph Palmer, John Guppell (£20)
**John Wattkins** (£50) - James Moore, Capt. Edmond Bellinger (£25)
**Joshua Wilkes** (£100) - John Alexander, David Maybanck (£50)
**Ralph Wilson** (£50) - Thomas Smith, George Dearsley (£25)
**Richard Abram** (£60) - William Popell, Nicholas Barlycorne (£30)
**Richard Newton** (£50) - George Dearsley, Edward Rawlins (£25)
**Robert Fenwick** (£60) - Sir Nathaniel Johnson, John Alexander (£30)
**Robert Matthews** (£60) - Anthony Shorey, Isaac Redwood (£30)
**Roger Clare** (£30) - Charles Basden, Henry Stillery (£15)
**Roger Goffe** (£40) - Major Robert Daniel, Chas Burnham (£20)
**Thomas Pinckney** (£60) - Sir Nathaniel Johnson, Francis Noble (£30)
**William Balloh** (£100) - John Sullivan, Edward Loughton (£50)
**William Crossbye** (£30) - Charles Basden, Henry Stillery (£15)
**William Walesby** (£60) - William Williams, John Lovell (£30)

Now its time to note a few things here regarding the above information. Of interest, the above being added as a curious bonus to the back of the book, the editor makes it known to the reader that this record was discovered with the *Journal* entries, but was attached with an index that indicates it once belonged to another volume.[7] Presumedly this other volume may have contained more information on Raynor and their depositions, but has conveniently and mysteriously been lost to time.

First of all, for those already well-versed in Charleston history, some of these names, of both the crew and those that backed them, likely stand out to you, and will be addressed when we discuss what became of the crew in the aftermath of their arrival. But it is apparent that since their brief time in Charles Town within the month, the crew independently crafted some strong bonds with the locals, many of them of high society - so strong of bonds that these Charles Town citizens literally and suddenly put their own finances on the line for these newcomers. It has long been suspected by historians that much occurred behind the scenes regarding these pirates and their treasures. You'll notice that a good deal of these people put stakes on not only a single member of the crew, but sometimes multiple crewmembers at once, and remember that £25 was about a year's wage for a physical labor job at sea. John Alexander, for example, was obviously more than convinced that these three strangers, Captain George Raynor, James Gillchriste, and Joshua Wilkes, wouldn't just up and leave. In fact, he was willing to gamble £350 on it. Agreeing with historians before myself, it's much easier to gamble when it's not your own finances at stake, or if you've been paid that amount or more "just in case." But reputations were also on the line - perhaps reputations costed a bit more. Lets examine briefly a few of these citizens.

(**Figure 16**: *"Engraving of an old portrait of Parliamentarian and colonial governor Nathaniel Johnson, 1644-1713"*)

The aforementioned John Alexander had immigrated to Charles Towne some time prior to 1691 and married Ann Axtel. Following the arrival of George Raynor's men and vouching for them, he became a landowner, and represented the Commons House of Assembly. After his passing, his wealthy widow would marry into the Boone family.[8]

Sir Nathaniel Johnson stood behind both Robert Fenwick and Thomas Pinckney, and had already been the owner of Silk Hope Plantation, yet rumors in the Leeward Islands persisted that he had been conspiring to betray Charles Towne to the French on behalf of James II. He had also been involved as a member of the Goose Creek Men; men who were notoriously at odds with higher ups of Charles Towne that lived just to the north inland along the Goose Creek - these men had gained notoriety for welcoming and dealing with pirates. When pirates would approach Charles Towne and were snubbed, they would venture further inland to contact and do dealings with the "much more reasonable" Goose Creek Men. Nathaniel Johnson had also opposed the prior governor James Colleton, and found comradery amid Seth Sothel, who again had a notorious criminal history. Despite all of this, in the aftermath, Johnson would go on to become the governor of South Carolina in 1703, his authority as which he would go on to use to benefit the previously mentioned Goose Creek Men.[9]

James Moore is another noteable name on this list, who stood by John Watkins as security. Barbadian-born, Moore had arrived to South Carolina in 1675 and became the leader of the political faction of the Goose Creek Men. He also supported the replacement of James Colleton with Seth Sothel; who when he arrived down from North Carolina allowed the Goose Creek Men the opportunity to seize power and drive Colleton out of the English colony. Elected as governor from 1700-1703, during 1702, he would partake in part of the conflict of the War of Spanish Succession, or, Queen Anne's War. This war saw England pitted against Spain, in which Moore used his political standing to lead the nautical assault against St. Augustine in Spanish-controlled La Florida. This effort was largely successful, and saw Moore leading his men to plunder the Spanish town, yet failed to overcome their fort, the Castillo de San Marcos, which ironically had been constructed to thwart would-be attempts by pirates after their own history of being pillaged prior. While the wealthy Moore would pass away in 1706 of yellow fever, his son James Moore Jr. would go on to serve as the governor of South Carolina from 1719-1721.[10] His other son, Roger Moore, would go on to later marry a girl named Mary Raynor; Captain George Raynor's soon-to-be-born daughter.[11]

Robert Gibbs, who backed crewmate Adam Richardson, was one of Charles Towne's initial settlers in the 1670s. Shortly after being involved with Richardson in 1692, he joined the First Commons House of Assembly, and six years later was appointed as a Proprietor's Deputy, got onto the Grand Council, and became Chief Justice in the same year.[12] In June 1710, he would be elected governor of South Carolina, though he was declared of being able to do so through illegal bribery.

Captain Edmond Bellinger, an alternate spelling of Edmund Bellinger, is another noteworthy name here who acted as security for John Wattkins. In 1698 Captain Bellinger, a noted friend of the Lords Proprietors, became a Landgrave, granted 13,000 acres known as the

## Charles Towne, South Carolina

Tomotley Barony at the locale of the swamp known as Tomotley; then-being noted as lands belonging to the native Yemassee people. In 1702 he would go on to attain 6,000 more acres at the head of the Ashepoo River.[13]

Joseph Palmer is a particularly interesting security name for two reasons. Joseph bears the same last name as crewmate John Palmer. While a familial tie is unproven, Joseph Palmer wouldn't be the only of this crew that had family in Charles Towne prior to their arrival, another being Daniel Hory (Horry). While the corrupt Sothel, hopefully still being in charge of the colony, may have swayed the votes of the crew to come to Carolina, Hory and Palmer's votes might have perhaps been due to knowing they would have family in Charles Towne who could harbor them, or provide financial or legal aid if need be. The second reason is the particular name, Joseph Palmer. It should be noted that a Captain John Palmer who was known to have been born in 1665 and lived out his life in the New England area with no known ties to piracy, and who also had a younger brother, Joseph Palmer, born in 1667.[14] This puts Joseph at about twenty-five years of age - a prime age for a sailor, though his location in 1692 is unknown. A Joseph Palmer does exist here in Charles Town in 1692, assisting crewmate John Palmer of the *Loyal Jamaica* after their piratical endeavors. Four years later in 1696, the famous Captain William Kidd would set sail as a legal privateer bound to hunt pirates such as Thomas Tew, and amid his crew was also an English sailor named Joseph Palmer. This Palmer is noteworthy as being one of the main two of Kidd's crew that testified against him at his later trial following his capture.[15] In 1717, twenty-five years later after Raynor's crew arrives, pirate Captain Stede Bonnet of the *Revenge* would capture a sloop just off the Cape Fear River along the Carolina coast - and it belonged to a Captain Joseph Palmer, who, like Bonnet, had originated from Barbados.[16] Integrating their tales however would be pure conjecture, and it is instead reported that the Joseph Palmer of Charles Towne was quite busy still in town during 1697, not off on escapades with Kidd, and is noted as being dead as of 1704, leaving behind his widow, Mary Palmer.[17] As odd as it is, there were indeed three separate Joseph Palmers, around the same time, and each of them interacted with three separate pirate crews, that of Raynor, Kidd, and Bonnet.

(**Figure 17**: *"Port Royal Earthquake of 1692," by Jan Luyken and Pieter van der Aa*)

With this all being said, these men who accompanied Raynor and testified to their innocence were not his entire crew. Varied reports state that the *Loyal Jamaica* arrived to Charles Towne with a crew of twenty-six; elsewhere its claimed forty,[18] another -seventy, and if you recall the records of Adam Baldridge he stated a crew of about seventy to eighty before they departed St. Mary's in Madagascar. The other thing to take into consideration here is we're also unaware of how many of these men had actually been pirates under Raynor, who of which were picked up while across the Atlantic, and which of them had perhaps committed piracy as members of other crews before and had joined Raynor's vessel on the way to Carolina. Although, again, the stops made were limited. Following the capture of Abdul Ghafur's ship in the Gulf of Aden, Raynor had taken his ship to Madagascar's island of St. Mary, allegedly being the first pirate to have spent time there, so it's fairly safe to say they didn't pick anyone up there. The next stop was Fort Dauphin, a native settlement, but one that a number of other sailors passed through and spent about a month there. The only two remaining stops were Ascension Island, which lacked fresh water; and the uninhabited Fernando Island. This is, of course, believing that the shipwrecked Danes spoke the truth about their voyage from their rescue to their arrival to Charles Towne.

Carrying on with the timeline, after Raynor and his men presented themselves, shortly afterwards on the 7th of June tragedy struck Port Royal, Jamaica, where he and his crew had departed long ago. Being a town positioned upon a long narrow peninsula in the harbor across from Kingston, it had long avoided natural disaster; this changed with a massive earthquake. The earthquake wrought devastation to the town, killing thousands and saw a tsunami crash over it. Port Royal was half submerged, ripped out into 40 feet of water, and the HMS *Swan* was lifted by the waves and crashed down atop a building. The island proved not to be made of bedrock, and the soil all but liquified.[19] The port was deemed uninhabitable, and corpses floated amid the building ruins. Even the buried remains of the famous Captain Henry Morgan was pulled out to sea and was never recovered. This event is important to the crew of Raynor, as this is relevant to the legal documentation of their ship.

The next event of note is that of the 11th of August regarding Mr. Robert Seabrooke, for whom modern-day Seabrook Island is named. Seabrooke was taken into custody and convicted for unlawful commerce with pirates that had arrived to his home, providing them with weapons and ammunition.[20] There is no further context for who these pirates had been, and this occurrence is not elaborated elsewhere, but it is likely that these were not the crew of Raynor; as they were still commonly known locally as "the privateers." This would not have been the first time a member of Charles Towne high society would collude with pirates, as a similar scenario took place about five years prior as well, concerning ex-Councilmember John Boone, of Boone Hall Plantation fame. Boone, in 1687, had been charged with collusion with the pirate Captain Henry Holloway, who had arrived prepared with an alibi that he had been trading with Spaniards. Instead, Holloway arrived to Boone and presented plundered goods in exchange for food and provisions, an unlawful deal that Boone was willing to engage with, resulting in his expulsion from the council.[21]

The Council of Charles Towne met again on the 22nd of August, discussing the departure of Captain William Pettit, who had since purchased the previously abandoned "*Loyal Jamaica*," and who had renamed her *Carolina Merchant*. Presumably after much repair and financial investment to get her back into working order for his means. Later during September, it was noted on the 15th that two of Raynor's crew attempted to flee Charles Towne during the latter days of August attempting to leave the province. These two men were Robert Fenwick, and Richard Newton who had been identified as their chirurgion, or surgeon, while at sea. They had attempted such by attempting to hitch a ride on Captain William Day's sloop *Dolphin* bound for New York, but fell victim to foul weather and were forced to return back to Charles Towne and fell into capture of the provost marshall. These men were both fined £500 each for the attempt. This would also mean that those who backed Fenwick as security, Sir Nathaniel Johnson and John Alexander would be forced to pay £30 each, as well as George Dearsley and Edward Rawlins £25 each for the escape attempt by Newton.[22]

It is also now, finally, that crewmates Henry Perry, Thomas Pinckney, Edmund Medlicotte, and Captain George Raynor deliver their depositions, their side of the story regarding their arrival in record. However, it seems that they likely already had appeared and delivered their story initially - these following depositions were put on record for the sole purpose of peace of mind for William Pettit, who owned their former ship, wanting it to be on record that the ship had been acquired legally before he would proceed to sell it once more, wishing to have no issues with the law himself. It was seen fit as a necessity, as the original records of the legal transfer of her to John Bell back in Jamaica in 1690 had since been lost with the destruction of Port Royal from the earthquake. The four crew who agreed to testify the legal transfer were, in order, Henry Perry, Thomas Pinckney, Edmund Medlicotte, and George Raynor. Their statements are as follows:

- Henry Perry; noted as being twenty-six years of age, told the council that he had been a crewmember of the *Dyamond* under Captain Thomas Harrison out of Port Royal, Jamaica, having signed on legally as a privateer against France. He then relays the capture of their vessel near Port de Paix, and bringing her back to Port Royal as a French prize where she was sold to John Bell and Company. He finishes the statement by admitting that she had been the same ship they'd arrived in, that had been taken by Charles Towne and condemned, and had been re-sold to Captain William Pettit and re-named currently as the *Carolina Merchant*.[23]

## Charles Towne, South Carolina

- Twenty-four year old Thomas Pinckney was next, relaying the exact same story, as did Edmund Medlicott, but stating that he'd originally been a member of the sloop *Mary* back in Port Royal with Raynor.

- Without adding any additional claims or information, Captain Raynor simply relayed the same statement for the record, that they had indeed taken her legally under the English flag "*near Portapee* [Port de Paix]" and took her to Port Royal. None of these men admitted in court during this time on record, of course, to their actions around the Indian Ocean and the Arabian Sea.[24]

On the 29th of September, a little over a month later, the records state that by Governor Ludwell's hand and seal, that the ship referenced by the prior deponents, those being the crew of the former *Loyal Jamaica*, had once again already changed hands. This time, the vessel, then-named *Carolina Merchant*, was re-sold by Captain Pettit to a man named Jonathon Amory and his associates.[25] Amory had originated from England, the son of a "merchant adventurer," and who had relocated to Barbados, and then again to Charles Towne in 1685 after the passing of his wife. In the colony, he served as the Speaker of the Assembly, Advocate-General, and Public Treasurer of South Carolina.[26] However, this is seemingly where the history of the former pirate ship ends. Amory would perish to yellow fever in 1699, and there is no further record of captaincy or further name changes, or what becomes of the vessel beyond his acquisition of her in late 1692.[27]

Also concerning the ownership of the vessel, while a date is not specified, in the later 1699 statement from Adam Baldridge of Madagascar regarding Raynor and the crew of the *Bachelor's Delight*, Baldridge would report that he had come into information that:

"*I have heard since they arrived at Carolina and Complyed with the owners, giveing them for Ruin of the Ship three thousand pounds, as I have heard since.*[28]"

This is believed to reference news later reaching Baldridge that Raynor and his men would have pooled together funds equaling 3,000 from their divided shares to send to the former owner, John Bell, from whom they had technically stolen his ship, did with it as they pleased, and ran her to a condemnable condition before it was confiscated. There is no official documentation of this transaction, but Baldridge also has no incentive or anything to gain by fabricating this hearsay either.

Most curiously, and to many historians over the years, suspiciously, somehow the cargo of the *Loyal Jamaica* was never declared or recorded by any individuals, neither upon their arrival, nor in the years following. Amid the records there is nothing to discover in the old microfilm probate records and inventories, no summaries from the *Calendar of State Papers*, and seemingly was unrecorded by customs collectors. This is also despite the fact that the Public Treasurer of South Carolina resulted in being the owner of the pirate vessel in the end. Still, the authorities certainly didn't give her crew much of a problem, and nearly immediately most of the "privateers" began purchasing massive plots of land, constructing plantations, purchasing their own ships, and integrating themselves into the most powerful and wealthiest families of Charles Towne. However, there is a statement by 18th century historian and author, Alexander Hewatt, who recited known information about the crew upon their arrival to the Carolina colony, stating with disdain that:

"...*the vessel was shipwrecked on the coast* [a reference to her condemnable condition], *the crew of which openly and boldly confessed, they had been in the Red Sea plundering the dominions of the Great Mogul. The gentleness of government towards those public robbers, and the civility and friendship with which they were treated by the people, were evidences of the licentious spirit which prevailed in the colony.*[29]"

Yet, in Hewatt's report, it would appear that already history had become somewhat muddied. While the above is certainly true, corroborated by compiled period accounts from across the world, Hewatt does mistake the occurrence of the arrival of the "*Royal*" *Jamaica*, consisting of forty crew said to have brought in Spanish plunder, with the arrival of other separate pirates arriving from the Red Sea, when in fact the two occurrences referenced are in fact one in the same when analyzed to the extent capable with tools and resources that are available to present-day researchers. During 1715, in *A Letter From South Carolina - Profitable*

*Advice for Rich and Poor*, Thomas Nairne discusses the sheer variety of coinage circulating throughout the colony - with foreign currency generally reigning predominent, stating:

*"Besides Bills of Credit, the Money most common in this Province is French Pistoles, Spanish and Arabian Gold...[30]"*

The author goes on to state in addition to those above, other prevalent currency in Carolina further consisted of Dutch and German Dollars, Peruvian and Mexican Pieces of Eight, and Spanish royals and half-royals. It is stated that amid the colony there is "very little English money.[31]" Another publication, *The Money Supply of the American Colonies Before 1720* by Curtis Nettels, published during 1934, discusses as the name implies currency about the colonies. In this work, he states in reference to the amount of highly valued pirated money in circulation that the economy of South Carolina's colony: *"For a time were flushed with Spanish silver and Arabian gold.[32]"*

As for any records of how the goods of Raynor's crew were traded and sold, they are non-existent. Most often pirates in possession of goods they should not have had often faced much difficulty in unloading said goods. In most cases, a fence or a "middle man" of sorts was required, who already had acquired a network of unscrupulous individuals with whom to export and import ill-gotten gains; contacts that the robbers themselves lacked. It is for this reason the success and necessity of "pirate havens" such as the later nest of pirates at Nassau in the Bahamas, Madagascar with Adam Baldridge, or, while not a "haven" in this context, even the Goose Creek Men of Goose Creek, South Carolina. These individuals, willing to work with pirates and act as brokers between clients, facilitated many transactions and the moving of pirated goods as private deals that managed to evade their way onto any written records. As such, documentation of the moving of Mughal treasures having arrived aboard the *Loyal Jamaica* may never come to light - as more than likely they do not exist.

Through personal research, no evidence or history of Mughal and Middle Eastern goods seem to arise in the present-day that may have ties to the 17th century event. The Gibbs Museum might perhaps be a lead, given its "Charleston Collects" series, in which private owners of art from the Charleston area put their own collections on display for the public. While not constantly on display, for the period of October 2018 - February 2019, the museum hosted a full display of Mughal artwork, from painting to sculptures, on loan by an un-named local collector. Of course there is no record of when these pieces first came to Charleston, if they were inherited, or how long they've been in the area, or if they were pieces simply accumulated from overseas and purchased more recently. It would be presumptuous to assume that any of these pieces, although dated to the period, could have been part of the undocumented cargo of the *Loyal Jamaica*.[33]

Lastly, two years would pass before the Council would report anything again regarding the case of the privateers and their vessel, *Loyal Jamaica*. It would be the final reported occurrence regarding the case. On the 22nd of February, 1694, it would be noted that:

*"Samuel Lowe and John Harris, of Port Royal, Jamaica, merchants, executed their bond in the sum of £1000. to George Rayner, of Carolina, merchant, indemnifying him from suits or actions by themselves or any of their agents, or from Thomas Harrison, formerly captain of the ship called the Loyal Jamaica, or any of his agents, by reason of his turning said Harrison out of his command of the said ship. Witnesses: Edward Shory, Samuel Sligh and Thomas Cumber. Proved by Sligh and Cumber before William Smith, March 30, 1694. Recorded by Paul Grimball, agent, April 6, 1694.[34]"*

In essence, this documentation alludes to a private deal handled outside of court, likely initiated by Raynor but involving himself, Thomas Harrison, and two potentially unscrupulous merchants located in Port Royal who would agree to protect Raynor financially leaving him unworried about his crew's past transgressions against Harrison when they tool the *Loyal Jamaica* two years prior. Essentially, Raynor likely brokered a deal privately where much coinage was in play, that benefited everyone involved.

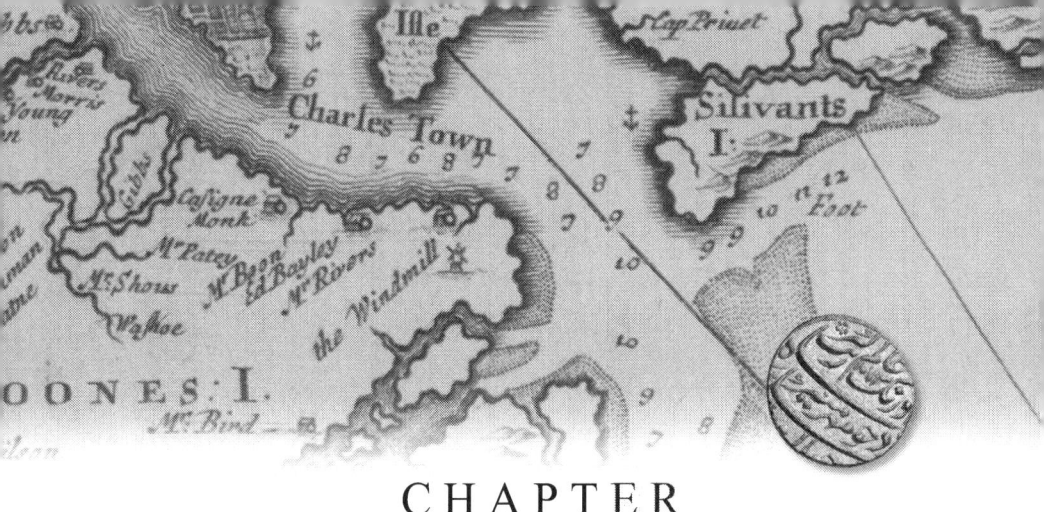

# CHAPTER
# Five

*The Red Sea Men Legacy*

It would seem that piracy really paid off, at least for the crew of George Raynor; which certainly was a rarity in their line of work. Many who turn to the trade often find themselves the victims of bad luck, or don't know when to stop, ultimately succumbing to greed; "Just one more job and then I'm out of the game…" Pirate Captain Henry Every may have secured a larger haul of treasure a few years later, but was forced into hiding. Raynor and his men did as they pleased, made their fortunes, arrived to Charles Towne, and got off the hook by throwing their bountiful riches towards the higher-ups with their hands out. These men went on to live their lives as if they'd done nothing wrong. In this chapter it is time to address the crew, their impact on Charles Towne and the surrounding regions, and how their arrival to Carolina's coast can still be felt today.

Richard Abram certainly remained in the Province of Carolina up until at least the end of 1693, as we have records of what he did with a portion of his money. On the 29th of December, he was noted as having purchased the ketch named *Elizabeth*, which he had renamed to the *Bristoll Ketch* and commanded now as captain.[1]

Adam Richardson, by the 20th of January, 1693, had already been wed to a girl named Mary, and had crafted his will designating her as the recipient of one-third of his fortune and estate. This was seemingly set up just in time, as by April 3rd, 1694, Richardson is noted as deceased.[2]

Christopher Linckley (Linkly) apparently had married into the Grimball family, wedding Ann Grimball, the daughter of wealthy English merchant Paul Grimball who had settled on Edisto Island. Upon Paul's death in late 1695, Christopher Linkly received the inheritance of four-hundred acres of land. He had also, in the years since his arrival, purchased and became captain of the sloop *Elizabeth*.[3]

Daniel Horry, his last name pronounced "O'Ree," had been one of perhaps only a few of the crew to have arrived to Charles Towne knowing he would be among his family, who were French Huguenot refugees who had emigrated to the port town in the early years of the 1680s. Daniel Horry was born in 1662 just outside of Paris, France, fleeing his home country with his brother Elias Horry sometime after 1686, bound for the Netherlands, and moving on from there to England.[4] Somehow, Horry ends up on the *Loyal Jamaica* before her arrival to Charles Towne six years later, perhaps the connecting point being a trip from England to Port Royal by 1690. The alternative would see Raynor picking him up… somewhere between the Red Sea and Carolina. Daniel Horry would marry Elizabeth Fanton Garnier in August after his arrival to Charles

(**Figure 18**: *"Peter Horry Canvas Painting,"* late 18th century)

Towne, and would pass away only three years later in 1696, being buried in Craven County, modern-day Horry or Marion County, but no known grave marker has been discovered.[5] He did leave behind a legacy however, as a descendant of his would arise and grow to fame. Peter Horry, born in 1743, would go on to make a name for himself during the American Revolutionary War alongside famed Brigadier General Francis Marion. It is for Daniel's descendant that Horry County, South

Carolina, is named, stretching from the area of Murrell's Inlet all the way to the North Carolina state line.[6]

Thus far unmentioned in this work, was another aboard the *Loyal Jamaica,* who doesn't appear in court records; that man being John Blackmore, who had been around since the beginning of the venture. While not among those who stepped forth to pay bail, Blackmore is later identified as having been a member of the crew years later by a proclamation put forth by the governor of Maryland on the 22nd of July, 1698. It is stated within the *Proceedings of the Council of Maryland, 1636-1770, Volume 23*, that a local sheriff of Ann Arundell County had captured two men, Mr. John Blackmore and a Mr. William Cotter on suspicion of piracy. It states:

*"...they say they went out of Jamaica under the Command of one George Rainer in a private man of war Commissionated by the Lord Inchequin then Governor of Jamaica, went from thence to the red Sea & returned to Carolina having been out near two Years from Carolina they went to Pensylvania & from thence they Came hither to Maryland in the Year 1692 in the time that Colonel Copley was Governor of this Province.[7]"*

The statement of their actions is followed by information of what they did with their Red Sea fortune after fleeing Charles Towne shortly after their arrival. Both men had settled in Ann Arundell County and purchased tobacco plantations and servants to work them. Blackmore also is regarded as a captain by this point, having come into the possession of a pink, a type of square-rigged cargo vessel, named the *Ann* by 1693. However, rather than face the harsh punishment often doled out to pirates, their crimes of piracy were simply dropped as they had proved to be good and honest members of their community since their arrival, with Cotter even being married with two children -by all appearances, a well-behaved family man. They were merely only asked to abide by the law and to appear if summoned, should ever their shrouded pasts be relevant, with a punishment to those acting as their separate securities being charged £500 each, if this was not obeyed.[8]

Another undocumented crewmate of Raynor's who is of interest and has not yet been mentioned; was a man named Richard Want. He also had not been reported as coming forth with the captain and his men to pay bail. As reported within the *Colonial Records* on the 9th of February in 1696, a letter from Whitehall states:

"Want, a Pyrate about three years ago, after a good voyage broke up in Carolina, and spent part of his money there. Want is now fitted out from Carolina. Pirates are kindly entertained in Carolina; Capt Risby and others of Every's Crew went to Carolina.[9]"

The mention of Captain Henry Every here is a connection between Raynor's voyage to the Red Sea and that of Every's later excursion; with Want being involved in both. After concluding his time with Raynor plundering in the Red Sea, Richard Want was certainly not finished with piracy, would not be content to retire in Charles Towne, and, no pun intended, -wanted more. Before the end of the year, while the men of the *Loyal Jamaica* were forbade from leaving the province, Want departed to join Bermudan privateer Captain Thomas Tew of the *Amity* on his December 1692 cruise to the Red Sea; ambitions perhaps driven by Raynor's apparent prior success. Richard Want had literally just done the route and eagerly signed on as his first mate. Want, captain of his own ship, the *Dolphin*, perhaps a Charles Towne purchase, ventured out yet again to the Red Sea and the two saw great success upon their return to Newport.[10] Not long afterwards, and undeniably being a man with an insatiable taste for adventure, or one of copius greed, Captain Want returned to the Red Sea for even more treasure in 1694, this time with both Tew and Henry Every. After their capture of the Grand Mughal's ship, the *Ganj-i-Sawai*, Want received a normal share, which even alone without the previous gains from the two endeavors with Raynor and Tew, would have made him fabulously wealthy.[11] After being dropped off in the Bahamas during 1696 as the crew of Every's *Fancy* scattered, Want arrived back in Charles Towne once more - apparently with no questions asked; and thus, settled down and married.[12] He wouldn't remain though, ultimately returning back to New England.

Regarding the above mentioned colonial records, it is worth taking note of the named Captain Risby, one of Every's pirates who had also settled down in Charles Towne quietly. By all accounts, it would seem the officials did not, or were paid not to, care about his line of work or the rest of his past. Prior to involvement with Every, Risby had quite the buccaneering career; from being a English logwood smuggler in 1669, operating on behalf of the Governor of Jamaica like Raynor had, to sailing alongside sieur de Grammont in 1684 in an attempted a piratical attack on St. Augustine, Florida. Later in 1702, Charles Towne even gave command of a naval force to Risby to sail against St. Augustine, a siege led by the governor as part of Queen Anne's War.[13] While there is no noted relations, Captain George Raynor certainly had some fellows in Charles Towne that he had quite a bit in common with. One may even speculate if Raynor and Risby had perhaps interacted with one another at some point in the years leading up to Raynor's mutiny in 1690. Captains are often elected following mutinies due to experience. Raynor was no newcomer to the sea life, and given his age he could have easily had a career of ten years at sea before 1690. However, this is pure conjecture.

Robert Fenwick is a name that might perhaps sound familiar, likely due to the still-standing Fenwick Hall near the Stono River on Johns Island. While the plantation home was built instead by his brother, John Fenwick in 1730, the home has never been able to escape its "association with pirate history" through its familial ties. After arriving aboard the *Loyal Jamaica*, Robert Fenwick did however marry into high society, to Sarah Patey, the daughter of Theophilus Patey - one of the richest men in the entire colony, and owner of the lands that Boone Hall Plantation would later be built upon. Robert also became a member of

(**Figure 19**: *"Fenwick Hall Plantation, Johns Island, Charleston County, South Carolina"*)

the Commons House of the Province.[14] With his older brother Robert now residing in the colony of Carolina, seemingly enjoying it as his new home, John shipped over from England in 1703 and then proceeded to serve as the Commissioner of the Indian Tract, overseeing uncolonized lands surrounding Charles Towne. In the 1720s, construction on the plantation and its property began. Unfortunately Robert wouldn't live to see its 1730 completion, passing away in 1727. Yet as a result of his arrival to Charles Towne as a Red Sea Man, Boone Hall was constructed, and grew into a massively successful source of rice. Of course, as rice production in Charles Towne increased, so too did the importation of enslaved Africans to work the fields.[15] Some of the tales associated with Robert Fenwick and Fenwick Hall will be relayed towards the end of this work, bookending the history of Charleston's Red Sea Men with their associated alleged local folklore.

Thomas Pinckney, crewmate of the *Loyal Jamaica*, is possibly the most important of her crew that arrived Charles Towne in 1692, at least in the context of the interactions of what his lineage would do for South Carolina. Soon after the pirates appeared, Thomas married Grace Bedon, and became a merchant of Charles Towne. While the 'official story', according to the Pinckney lineage, is that Thomas came to Carolina with a mere £150, he quickly obtained ownership of a mercantile business, purchased multiple lots within the town, owned over four-hundred and eighty acres along the eastern banks of the Ashepoo River, and established his home with a wharf that is now 57 East Bay Street. He rapidly became one of the most wealthy businessmen in the colony. This was on top of his fines, living expenses during his home's construction, and the cost of building materials as well. Pinckney most certainly arrived with substantially more loot than is generally told. He would also go on to re-marry, namely the daughter of Charles Cotesworth, Mary.[16] It is from these marriages that Pinckney sets forth a long line of noteworthy descendants. These include, in order:

Charles Pinckney (1699-1758): Chief Justice of the South Carolina Supreme Court. Colonel Charles Pinckney (1732-1782): President of the South Carolina Provincial Congress, owner of Snee Farm Plantation; modern-day Charles Pinckney National Historic Site in Mt. Pleasant SC. Charles Cotesworth Pinckney (1746-1825): signer of the Constitution of the United States, associate of George Washington, nearly President of the United States in 1808, and namesake for Pinckneyville SC. Thomas Pinckney (1750-1828): Governor of South Carolina and US Envoy to Spain. Charles Pinckney (1757-1824): signer of the Constitution of the United States, Governor of South Carolina.[17]

(**Figure 20**: *"General Charles Cotesworth Pinckney, 1796," by James Earl*)

Further descendants from Charles Pinckney (1757-1824) would go on to serve as seven more future South Carolina governors. Indeed an impressive legacy for Thomas, who established multi-generational wealth from both piracy in the Red Sea, and his affluent marriage match. His participation and arrival aboard the crew of the *Loyal Jamaica* truly impacted and shaped the history of South Carolina, and the United States, going forward.

William Balloh, whose name can also be found in various documents as "Ballough" or "Bollough," would go on to settle along the Wando River, near an area called Wappetaw, the lands of which sat between modern-day Ayer's Point and Wando Farms. His eventual descendants would marry into the Edens family, as well as the Dorril or "Dorrell" families, of modern-day Dorrell Creek Community.[18]

## ANALYSIS OF CAPTAIN GEORGE RAYNOR

Before addressing Raynor's lasting impact, lets briefly examine his origins. Prior to being a crewmate aboard the *Mary* in Port Royal, Raynor is said to have been born in or about 1659/1660 in Bishopsgate, London, which indeed puts him about the noted age of thirty-four for the arrival to Charles Towne in 1692.[19] This origin is noted on the website Ancestry, mentioned in the entry for his eventual wife, Dorcas Davis. Examination into this claim eventually led to the discovery in *The Registers of St. Botolph, Bishopsgate, London*, an Anglican church in London, - the birth of George Rayner. He was born in January 1659, to parents George Rayner and Rachel Rayner, maiden name Rachell Lucock, the two of whom had married in 1656 in Westminster.[20] There is also, according to *The Registers of St. Helens Bishopsgate, London*, a nearby church of Bishopsgate, a noted marriage between that of Will Howe of Feltsteed and maiden Sara Rayner of Darford during 1651. What this does show is that a Rayner family did exist in the vicinity of Bishopsgate, London, extending at least as far back as the mid-17th century.[21] Further evidence of the Rayner family are the numerous documented Rayner family graves prior to 1700 around Yorkshire north of London, and a number within London as well, including that of Captain Raynor's father, George Rayner Sr.; who passed away on April 9th, 1688, and was buried in the Old Chiswick Cemetery.[22] Also please recall once again, as stated prior in this work, that I the author have continued using the more commonly used modern "Raynor" for this work despite the various spellings that occur throughout reports; however, "Rayner" does seem to be the prevalent spelling of the period.

This puts George Raynor Jr. growing up as a child in London during the 1660s, where at ages five through six this child would have bore

(**Figure 21**: *"The Thames in the 17th Century," which depicts a view of the river looking in the direction toward Southwark Cathedral, by Duncan Harris, 2012*)

witness to the bubonic Great Plague - the worst plague outbreak since the Black Death. While unsure of the social class of his parents, those in the city proper suffered less, while suburban parishes on the fringes and along the Thames River suffered most. This outbreak led to many, who could afford it, to emigrate away from London. It is my personal theorization that young Raynor and his family did not relocate due to his father's burial in London later in 1688, and his mother's death circa 1701 there as well. As a child here, Raynor would have been around for the loss of about twenty-five percent of the population of London from the plague.[23] This event was immediately followed up, or, concluded by, The Great Fire of London, which occurred during 1666. During which, a total of 13,200 homes and 87 parish churches were decimated.[24] It is unknown how this young lad transitioned into a sailor later working in the vicinity of Jamaica, but he would have been located near the Thames River with a bustling port scene. After a few more years, Raynor could have easily found his way to sea during the late 1670s or during the 1680s, as the Thames River was a prime location of legal privateers sailing out to partake in the ongoing Nine Years War, their commissions of which often saw these ships sailing out against France and Spain, and heading to the Caribbean.

Following his later piratical adventure to the Red Sea, and once Raynor was settled into Charles Towne, during 1693 he is noted as spending his wealth purchasing three plots of land within the town proper.[25] The following year, a woman named Dorcas Davis, born in 1675, at nineteen years of age would become the object of affection for Captain Raynor in 1694. She would soon become impregnated, and shortly after the two wed the following year, Dorcas gave birth to their only daughter, Mary Raynor during 1695 or 1696.[26]

Also during 1695, Raynor would be noted as being assembled among a committee alongside Mr. Gabriel Glaze and Captain Edmund Bellinger. The group had been picked by the Commons House to plan and discuss the concept of fortifying Charles Towne going forward. Upon discussion, the three would return the following day with their conclusion - that it would cost about £1,000 to *"make a regular and defencive ffortification at the end of the Broad Streete at the place called Southells ffort."* This "fort" oddly absent from most all records,

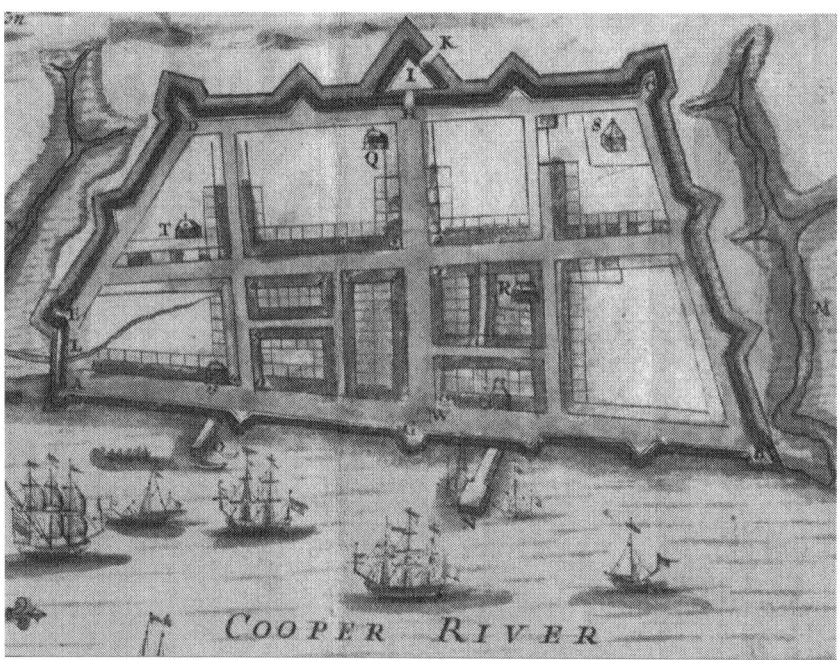

(**Figure 22**: *Cropped portion of the "Crisp Map of Charleston in 1711," with 'G' on the map indicating the Half-Moon Battery and modern-day site of the Old Exchange Building & Provost Dungeon*)

seemingly existed where the modern-day Old Exchange Building & Provost Dungeon now sits, which back then would have been the wooden Watch House.[27] This mention is following the June 1694 Wharf Act, in which orders were issued to construct a brick wharf wall along East Bay Street, beginning at the location of the Misroon House. It is believed that in prior years, perhaps during governorship of Seth Sothel, a half-moon shaped extension of poor materials had stood at the site of the Watch House. It is likely that what Raynor advocated for was the construction of the more legitimate and defensible "Half Moon Battery" to protect the Charles Towne Harbor. This fortification was completed, and nowadays a portion of it can still be seen from within the dungeon below the Old Exchange, which was later built atop the site replacing the wooden Watch House.[28]

After divorcing from Raynor for unspecified reasons, Dorcas would re-marry soon afterwards to Samuel Eveleigh, around the year 1698. Curiously, she is then addressed as the widow of George Raynor, which may have been misconstrued by the author of *A History of the Heverly Family...*, as Raynor would certainly be alive and well for at least a few more years doing some noteable things in the Charles Towne area.[29]

During 1699, Captain Raynor would make some very flashy purchases with his fortune. These included a total of 1,020 acres of property along the western side of the Stono River, and an unspecified island on the east side of the same river.[30] These acres of land would be upon modern-day John's Island, and while the smaller isle is not mentioned by name, it could possibly be (as they are currently known) Fiddler Island, Sol Legare Island, or either of the Coles islands amid the marsh. Yet most impressively, and most famously, is Captain George Raynor's acquistion of the entirety of Kiawah Island, a barrier island south along the coast from Charles Towne, and noted on most period maps as "Kayawah;" all 2,700 acres of it.[31] The island at the time had been a natural land of cattle cultivation and home to the Kayawah native Americans, and Raynor purchased the isle for a grand total of £54.[32] Despite ownership of the island, there is no stated record of Raynor ever having lived upon it, he instead likely stayed at his home on John's Island or downtown.

In early 1701 George Rayner seemingly grew concerned for his well-being, or simply proactively began growing concerned about what

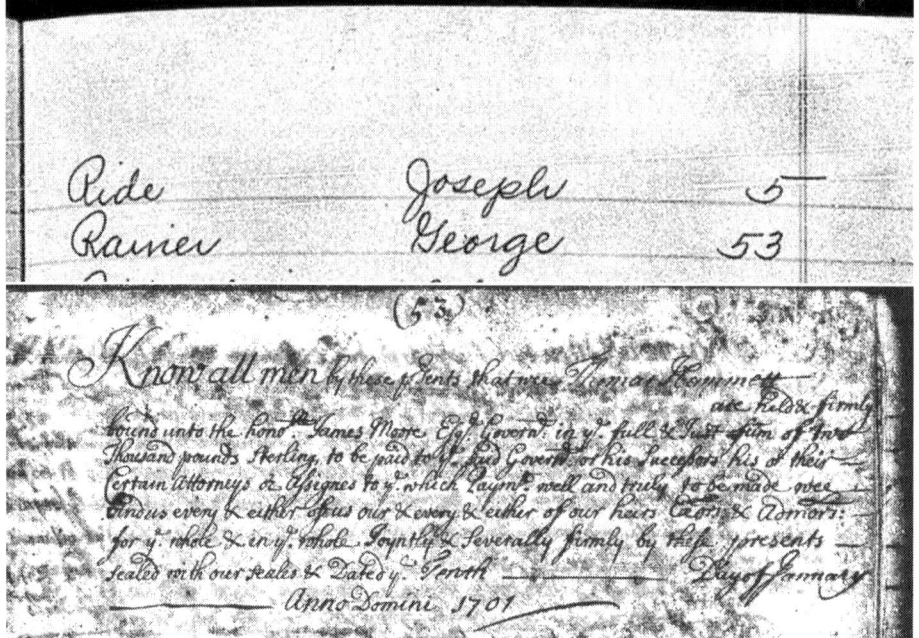

(**Figure 23**: Cropped portion of *"George Rainer Entry in directory, and accompanied Raynor Will, Entry 53"* in the *"South Carolina, U.S., Wills and Probate Records, 1670-1980"*)

would become of his possessions should something happen to him. On the 10th day of January, he created his will, recorded within Charleston's *South Carolina, U.S., Wills and Probate Records, 1670-1980*, recorded within by the record keeper as "George Raynor," and within the compilation of scanned documents is an accompanying book acting as a directory of entries - in which the associated Raynor's page is noted as "George Rainer" by another author with different handwriting.[33] Mysteriously, his belongings were largely to be left behind to a man named Thomas Haminett.

Later in the year, realizing he'd not needed all of Kiawah or perhaps simply wanting to flip the property to profit, on the 1st of November, 1701, he sold half of the island to a local named Captain William Davis. The remaining half he'd left as an inheritance to his daughter, Mary.[34]

As for what became of Raynor beyond this transaction exists only in speculation as his historical paper trail goes cold. As previously mentioned in this chapter, Captain Risby, a fellow former pirate would be placed in charge of a naval force of experienced individuals to lay siege to St. Augustine in 1702 - it would be comforting to imagine Raynor "coming out of retirement" as one of the roughly 500 Charles

Town colonists who took part in the endeavor and taking to the sea once more, with his knowledge and expertise shouted above the waves as cannonfire rocked his ship as his men let loose another broadside toward the Spanish ships… Exciting indeed, but this would be pure conjecture. By the 1720s Mary would move away to North Carolina, and would later pass the island she'd already inherited to her son. It's reasonable to presume that George may have passed by 1720, which would have seem him at around age 60.

For Raynor, a burial site is not mentioned, but reasonably, unless some new period account emerges to state otherwise, it can reasonably be assumed he lived out his life in Charleston until his end. From an analysis of all surrounding period graveyards and cemeteries, there appears to be no burial stone for Raynor or any other variation of its spelling. It is this author's belief that either the stone has been lost to time, or more likely the pirate captain was instead buried at a private residence, perhaps upon his property on Johns Island.

Raynor's ex-wife, Dorcas, was said to have passed away around April or May during 1715, but not before allegedly giving birth to two more children, each of whom would have been half-siblings to Mary Raynor. These included Samuel Eveleigh, Jr., in 1710, and Elizabeth Eveleigh in 1713.[35]

(**Figure 24**: *"Kiawah Island, SC, USA," photography by 'olekinderhook'*)

Lastly, Mary Raynor, became married to the incredibly wealthy Roger Moore; the son of future governor James Moore. Mary Moore relocated in 1723 further up along the Carolina coast with her husband to the area of the lower Cape Fear River, around the area of Brunswick. In 1737, upon her passing, ownership of Kiawah Island passed to her son, George Moore, named perhaps after her father. From up in North Carolina, the isle was sold, and eventually became known for its indigo plantations, followed by production of both rice and cotton.[36] Today, George Raynor's island has since seen major commercial development beginning in the 1950s, and now has been reshaped into a vacation island and home to the highly wealthy, covered with resorts, golf courses, and luxurious gated private communities. Due to its longshore current, rather than facing erosion in the years since pirate-ownership, the island instead has accumulated more sand and has only grown in mass, resulting in significant changes when comparing with period maps. [37]

## HOW WAS IT ALL PERCEIVED?

Knowing how successful this turned out for, well, seemingly most individuals that were involved, how did the other colonies feel about this outcome? What of England's thoughts on the matter?

Well, this wasn't the first case of the colony supporting piracy. The arrival of the *Loyal Jamaica* was a very blatant scenario that everyone amazingly allowed to happen, but Charles Towne, under the governorship of Seth Sothel or not, already had an existing reputation. The colony, established in 1670, spent its early years as a struggling port town that had a hard start staying afloat financially. As historian Eugene Sirmons once summed up:

*"...many of the pirates had been privateers during the conflicts with Spain and Anglo-Dutch wars of the 1660s and 1670s, and after the wars they had stepped over the thin line between privateering and piracy. Such men had nearly always been welcome in the colonies, because their raids had been traditionally against the Spanish and because they paid for their supplies in gold and silver. Several South Carolinians - most of them Barbadians - had discovered the profits in the pirate trade, and Charles Town had become a frequent port of call for the freebooters.*

## The Red Sea Men Legacy

*When the Lords of Trade first inquired about the trade in 1684, the proprietors tried to deny its existence.*[38]"

The arrival of the *Loyal Jamaica* and Raynor's crew would later go on to be surmised by historian Shirley Hughson in the 1890s as to how it had really been, although the crew number is unfounded:

*"A crew of forty men arrived in a vessel called the Loyal Jamaica, bringing with them large quantities of silver and gold. By means of their wealth they found immediate favor with many of the people, and the officials were so far swayed by considerations of which history does not speak, that they were permitted to remain in the Province unmolested.*[39]"

Even as immediately within the year of the arrival of the crew, legal action was taken to seemingly protect them and their wealth they brought to the colony. In September of 1692, a new bill was introduced, in response to being unable to provide the pirates pardons for their actions, which essentially granted complete indemnity to all pirates and their accomplices. Being a subject of fierce debate, the governor was forced to shut down the bill, but the result was a law put in place giving "colonial magistrates the power to enforce the English Habeas Corpus Act." This allowed the otherwise 'deemed criminals' to dispute the claims against them, challenging their imprisonment and legality of their capture and a demand for proof. The result of this saw many pirates simply taking up residence in the colony.[40]

During 1701, following the acts of piracy and capture of the pirate Captain William Kidd; Pennsylvania's governor, William Penn, would write to the Board of Trade with his suspicions regarding the colonies of Massachusetts, Maryland, New York, New Jersey, Virginia, and Carolina. He purported that each had been harboring pirates of Kidd's crew, making specific mention to call out Carolina based on their recent history, exclaiming in contempt that even: *"there Captain one Reiner now lives.*[41]" It wasn't uncommon for colonial governors to call out other colonies, often ratting out piratical interactions back to England, but the Carolina colony of Charles Towne received many accusations over the years, and rightfully so.

While still under governorship of Ludwell, many spoke of the alleged flagrant bribery in the jury-room, and after many complaints from the citizens, found it necessary to annul a particular law. It had been in place regarding the election of members of the Assembly, a local branch of government established by the people. At the time of the arrival of the *Loyal Jamaica*, the act was:

*"So loose in its construction that 'all the Pyrates that were in the Shipp that had been plundering in the Red Sea had been qualified to vote for Representatives.' The only requirement was that the voter should possess ten pounds, or property valued at that amount, and the pirates with their stolen gold were thus qualified as fully as the oldest free-holder in the colony.*[42]*"*

This complaint was likewise stated by those of the French Huguenots who had come to the Carolina colony in search of religious freedom. They found themselves here in their new home, yet persecuted against until 1693, stating the absurdity that they lacked the same rights as the seafaring criminals that had arrived from the Red Sea after plundering ships.[43]

Governor Ludwell's successor, Thomas Smith, during 1693, had been appointed to succeed against the pirates where Ludwell had failed. To the dismay of both proprietors and the people, Smith resigned from his position as governor, unwilling to contend with the tumultous situation. If the reports are to be believed, and not to be exaggerations meant to be demonize the newcomers, the pirates were claimed to be preparing "to attempt the plundering and burning of" Charles Towne. These accusations of course turned out to be nothing. The Red Sea Men were already content, already integrated into colonial life, and bore no ill intent on what was now their own home.[44]

In 1696 Edward Randolph arrived. He was a colonial administrator out of England, who made occasional visits to the colonies over in America to make sure that all was well. He became particularly well-known for writing back home, furiously, after visiting almost every colony, sending many scathing reports of how things were transpiring. His visit to Charles Towne of course was no different. His letters back across the Atlantic stated:

*"About three years ago seventy pirates, who ran away with a vessel from Jamaica, came to Charleston with a vast quantity of gold from the Red Sea. They were entertained, and had liberty to stay or go to any other place."*

Randolph's letter would go on to state that even the way the officials had gone about the seizure and sale of the pirates' ship was done in known violation of the Acts of Trade, and for their own personal profit, and had done so choosing to not alert the Crown's appointed tax collector. For his report, he arrived to the conclusion that the political leadership here both socially accepted and profitted from pirates.[45]

In time, and with enough subsequent complaints, England would force the colony to adhere to law, and after so many years finally crackdown on the crime of piracy. While no names are mentioned, eight pirates were hanged during the year 1700 as a turning point in their history, the act most likely carried out to appease England's demands. These hanged men were unlikely associated with the *Loyal Jamaica* in any way, but they were noted during 1700 by a letter written by Edward Hyrne. In the letter, addressed home to his wife, he spoke of his time in Charles Towne and of the terrible hurricane that befell the port on the 3rd of September. During the storm, which broke apart many ships that were cast upon the shore, a brigantine of about 80 tons had been thrown ashore at Oyster Point or the White Point, and in doing so busted down two sets of erected gallows from which eight pirate corpses had been hanged.[46]

Even the colony's 1702 assault against St. Augustine had been in the name of piracy. James Moore's attack against the Spanish port had been in retaliation, as the Spanish Empire had threatened Charles Town because they were well-known to support piracy. One man named John Ash even spoke out in criticism of the act afterwards, comparing it to piracy itself, and stating that Moore's attack was simply but:

*"A Project of Freebooting under the specious Name of War… with hopes of mighty Plunder.[47]"*

Charles Town would see a distance between themselves and pirates for some time, with the eruption of the War of Spanish Succession, or Queen Anne's War, which saw many of the English pirates legally employed throughout its run as legal privateers more concerned with Spanish targets such as those sailing out of Florida. In the aftermath however, as most naval conflicts concluded, the seas were once more filled with trained and successful sailors, skilled at taking down naval targets - only now they weren't allowed to legally. This of course led to the next burst of Caribbean piracy, from the likes of which spawned the next wave of many famous pirates such as Benjamin Hornigold,

Blackbeard, Stede Bonnet, Jack Rackham, Charles Vane, Samuel Bellamy, and many more. Once May of 1718 came about, Blackbeard blockaded the harbor, threatening to level the colony with cannonfire unless his demands were met - a heavy chest of medicine for he and his men. Ultimately, the port provided the requested medicine.[48]

This in turn saw pirates viewing Charles Town as a port that caved to pirate demands, which led to assaults by Charles Vane, George Lowther, and Richard Worley at the port before Charles Town would make a final statement against pirates- the execution of the captured Captain Stede Bonnet, the "Gentleman Pirate." Between the captured men of Worley's Crew, as well as Bonnet and his crew who had been captured in the Cape Fear river by pirate-hunter William Rhett, Charles Town would hang forty-nine pirates by the end of 1718, at the White Point, near modern-day White Point Gardens. This being said, the people of Charles Town had been sympathetic to Bonnet, and protested his execution.[49]

The Golden Age of Piracy as we now refer to it would largely draw to a close by 1730, with many stating 1718 to be the beginning of the end. Still many continued on piratical voyages away from the Caribbean, back to the Indian Ocean and operating where the Red Sea Men had been. While piracy was essentially "stomped out" of the Caribbean and Americas, they had simply relocated. A few individuals stepped up to continue running Madagascar's pirate haven after Baldridge's departure, and to this day the waters around Somalia and the Red Sea remain notorious for modern-day piracy.

For the most part, this closed Charleston's chapter regarding pirates, but no matter how many attempted to sweep their dealings away into obscurity, Charleston remained infamous ever after as having been a "pirate port."

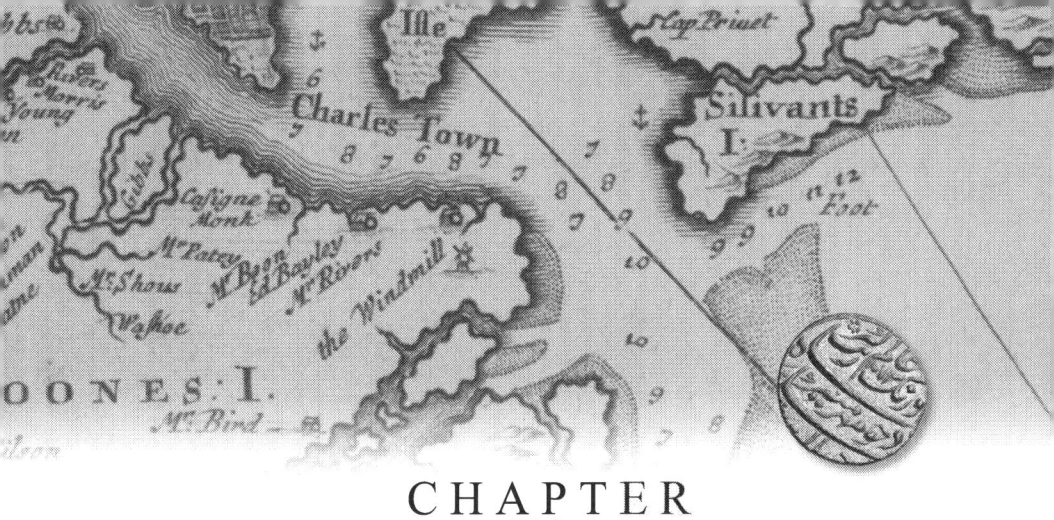

# CHAPTER
# Six

*The Muddled Mess & Common Presumptions,*

Regarding the overall history of Charleston's "Red Sea Men," there are quite an admittedly large amount of misconceptions, and incorrect historical accounts repeated ad-nauseum. This chapter serves to focus on the common misconceptions regarding the tales of the crew of the *Loyal Jamaica/Bachelor's Delight*, the things often incorrectly associated with her crew, and the folklore tales about them that have been perpetuated by Chareston locals over the past few centuries.

### GEORGE/JOSIAH RAYNOR

One of the most problematic assumptions, that has led to much confusion between the alleged tangled web of Raynor, Thomas Tew, and the vessel Bachelor's Delight, stems from a misunderstanding that George Raynor and Josiah Raynor are the same individual, utilizing the name George and Josiah interchangably. They are, in fact, separate men that confusingly both turned to piracy around the same time independently of each other.

First, we'll acknowledge that all primary source materials exclusively refer to the Charles Town Raynor as George, never once as Josiah. It has also been covered the birth of George Raynor/Rayner - Bishopsgate, London, UK in 1659/60, who arrived to Charles Towne in 1692 at the age of about 34, with a realistically timed alleged death of about 1720 or so. Now, as for the other American-born Josiah Raynor, he was born on February 8th, 1665 in Southampton, Suffolk, New York, with his father being Joseph Raynor and his mother being Mary Youngs. Josiah also has a more well-documented death date of October 19th, 1727.[1] Now Josiah Raynor is also known to have married a woman named Sarah W. Higby in 1687 in Lyme, Connecticut, to whom he returns to after his bout of piracy.[2] This younger Raynor was also busy welcoming into the world his Son Uriah Raynor, who was birthed in Southampton during 1692, while George Raynor and company were arriving in Charles Towne and interacting with the Council.[3]

The tales of Josiah Raynor's pirate adventure is often mistaken as an extension of George Raynor's. Josiah Raynor is noted as being along with pirate Captain Thomas Tew of the *Amity* in 1694, a voyage to the Red Sea with Henry Every.[4] While Thomas Tew is killed during this trip assaulting Mughal ships, Josiah Raynor eventually makes it back to New York around the year 1700 and was, rightfully, suspected of piracy and imprisoned by High Sheriff Josiah Hobart. To further reinforce this is a different Raynor; during this same time period, as previously mentioned, George Raynor was busy in Charles Towne getting married to Dorcas Davis, and going on record for the construction of a fortification for Charles Towne. Back up north, through pulling of social strings via his friend John Wicks, who gifted the governor fifty pounds; Governor Benjamin Fletcher released Josiah Raynor and the chest of treasure he had returned with - which was said to have belonged to Thomas Tew. The chest of now resides in the St. Augustine Pirate & Treasure Museum in St. Augustine, Florida. While Josiah is being captured and imprisoned, George is in Charles Towne buying and selling Kiawah Island and establishing his will. Upon Josiah

(**Figure 25**: *"Thomas Tew Chest, St. Augustine Pirate & Treasure Museum," photography by Adam Morrow*)

Raynor's release, he then settles in Lyme, Connecticut until his eventual death, allegedly around 1743 after having many more children - Adam, Deborah, Diademia, Elishebe, Ebenezer, Jessie, John, Joseph, Josiah II, Samuel, Sarah, and Siuell.[5]

## JAMES KELLY'S DEPOSITION

Of all pieces of the history of Captain George Raynor, the re-named *Bachelor's Delight*, and her return to the Carolina coasts - the pirate James Kelly consistently is the only problematic individual, who directly conflicts many of the otherwise first-hand period sources. If Kelly's 1700 deposition is to be believed with no questions asked, the result is all other primary sources to collectively be mistruths, unless we can figure out how he fits in. The alternative is that Kelly himself has a variety of fabrications within his deposition while on his deathbed. So, while the entirety of this publication you have read up to this point is purely factual and true, corroborated by countless period sources - aside from this one - what would it take to be true, if we were to believe the Deposition of James Kelly? Well first, let's analyze what Kelly said had happened.

*"...So I shipt myself a Privateer, Captain Thomas Harrison Commander: but he and his people not Agreeing, they would not go where he would have them, they having some shares in the Ship, would go where they Pleased.[6]"*

This is in reference to the re-launch of the former ship, *La Constance*, then re-named the *Loyal Jamaica*, under the captaincy of Harrison. According to Kelly, Captain Harrison allowed them to have the ship, departing from the flotilla aboard the sloop *Dyamond* - rather than being put ashore and degraded, as otherwise stated. Then, he states the crew sailed to Madeira, only taking provisions, just north of the Canary Islands. In the account, which so far has only differed that Harrison departed and was not otherwise "put ashore," Kelly states they next went to the Canaries and enacted all the events as previously described. The pirates, according to Kelly, then departed for the Cape Verde isles, and from there, following their visit to the isle of Fogo, were bound for Madagascar - which is where his allegation takes a turn…

Kelly confusingly claims a whole separate story from this point forward, stating a whole slew of adventures that take the supposed crew about the Indian Ocean, interacting with Captain William Kidd and referencing Kidd's crew going aboard the ship *Mocha* - a factual event that transpired much later in 1698, long after Raynor and company had already arrived to Charleston.[7]

Kelly closes his final deposition that he desired for his paper to be published and printed, to *"Prevent all false and Sham Accounts that may (perhaps) be set forth"* in his name, stating that he was the *"unfortunate"* and wishing that his fate be a warning to other seamen and notorious pirates. Kelly would be hanged the following day in London, July 12th, 1700, for his crimes of piracy on the high seas.

Kelly's reflection on his life, when compared to many other sources, is seemingly incorrect more often than it is corroborated. This can be chalked up to a few things. Take note that Kelly is a man facing certain death within the coming hours, frantically leaving behind a story; and that in other similar situations, pirates had been known to get off the hook -so to speak- if their story seemed marketable and warranted further elaboration for a book deal; James Kelly might have been simply playing up his life in efforts to appease listeners. Another possibility is that much was lost in translation, from the words he rambled off and that which was recorded by whoever was listening to his tale. In any case, the simplest answer, which is often the most correct, is that Kelly was making reference to a crew separate from that of the *Bachelor's Delight*. Nowhere in Kelly's period deposition does he mention being the Captain of the *Bachelor's Delight*, nor does he refer to her, nor George Raynor, by name. In this speculation of what may have transpired, after their departure from the island of Fogo, Kelly may have opted to leave the ship somewhere along Madagascar's shores. The isle as a whole was far from uninhabited; conversely, it was filled with shipwrecked sailors, and indigenous folk who often traded with sailors that came ashore. It requires no big stretch of imagination to presume that Kelly could have left the isle yet again after allowing Raynor to carry on as captain going forward, watching as the *Bachelor's Delight* dipped below the horizon and out of his sight. We don't know if Raynor and company would have visited Madagascar before hitting the Red Sea, we only have confirmation that Raynor and the *Bachelor's Delight* did visit the particular isle of St. Mary's afterwards.

The other possibility, is that yes, perhaps everything Kelly states was true as well, with his mention of Madagascar meaning the verified stop at St. Mary's, departing from the crew with his share of treasure while at Baldridge's haven following their escapades in the Red Sea, but not agreeing with the decision to sail for Carolina to retire. From here, it's even easier for Kelly to find a new ride to depart and continue his so-called career.

I would argue that the Deposition of James Kelly isn't so problematic, just that it's admittedly vague as to how he fits into the story of Raynor and the *Bachelor's Delight*. But we do know that he had been part of the *Dyamond*, had potentially served as a captain of the *Bachelor's Delight*, at least while en-route to the coast of West Africa, and reached Madagascar before seemingly departing for his own continued adventures in the region, while the rest of the crew certainly went to Charleston and had their own accounts separated from him across the world during those same years.

## BACHELOR'S DELIGHT & BATCHELOR'S DELIGHT

Most of the actual problems surrounding James Kelly and the history of George Raynor and the *Bachelor's Delight* stem from a common misconception not stated by period sources. This, of course, is the confusion that the *Loyal Jamaica/Bachelor's Delight* of 1690 forward, is the same famous *Batchelor's Delight* from years prior, whose crew included William Dampier, Lionel Wafer, Edward Davis, and to make matters worse - James Kelly.

The *Batchelor's Delight*, usually spelled exclusively with the "tch" in her name, had been a large Danish vessel captured by pirate Captain John Cook and company along the western coast of Africa in 1683, which they named as such and fitted her to be a man of war.[8] There is a perpetuated speculation that she may have perhaps been the former HMS *Portsmouth*, which had been previously captured by Dutch privateers in the prior decade, however this supposition lacks a period source. Following the death of Cook from illness, crewmate Edward Davis had been elected her captain. Much piracy was done with Captain Davis in control, but ultimately culminated with his capture in 1688 while in Virginia.[9] This is the last known location of the *Batchelor's Delight*.

As mentioned within this book's early pages, the *Bachelor's Delight* of Raynor's time had been the name given to the *Loyal Jamaica*, which before had been, according to French records, a French vessel named *La Constance*, out of La Rochelle, which had potentially been a frigate or ketch. In the time since the arrival of the "privateers" in Charleston, word of mouth local lore claims she had been a ketch as well.

Simply because of the name of Raynor's ship, and the association of James Kelly, many have presumed it to be the same, but more than likely the mutineers, including Kelly, opted to rename the *Loyal Jamaica* to that of "his old ship" where his prior career of piracy had left off. Or again, they collectively might have voted for its name, as the original had built quite a formidable reputation for itself as a pirate vessel under Cook and Davis. This also wouldn't be the first time similarly named things occurred around the same time either. We've already addressed the two Raynors, both of whom committed piracy "around" the same time, at the same region. Likewise, there were two *Bachelor's Delight*s, that of the 1680s, and that of the 1690s. One might even think of Raynor's as *Bachelor's Delight II*. Because of these presumptions, most history elongates the stories of Cook's *Batchelor's Delight* until nearly 1700, inserting generalizations and assumed fixes without primary sources to have it all make sense. These presumptions often state that the ship, after the capture of Davis, was later re-sold to her crew, and that she was taken on subsequent adventures into the Indian Ocean with Raynor and Kelly. This is also where an un-verified source once stated that George Raynor had previously been a member of Davis's crew on her during the 1680s.

The only way for this statement to be true, that the two ships are in fact one and the same, is for the Danish *Batchelor's Delight* to have been confiscated in 1688 by English forces, only to then fall into control of the French and become re-named to *La Constance*, only to then coincidently fall back into the lap of "two of her former crew" within two years, and was then subsequently granted her same previous pirate-given name, again.

These claims of both ships being the same, as well as Raynor's prior involvement, and also an earlier adventure taking place in 1689 or 1688 instead, were seemingly popularized in author Jan Rogozinski's history book, *Honor Among Thieves: Captain Kidd, Henry Every, and the Pirate Democracy in the Indian Ocean*, which was published in the year 2000. The book draws all the aforementioned suppositions together into a seemingly tight narrative, that has since gone on to become an oft-cited source regarding most all tales of the *Batchelor's Delight*'s history. One will note that all of these suppositions in Rogozinski's work that cobble together the ship's history, each mysteriously lack their sources, and others within that do include them simply refer back to 1953's *Piracy was a Business*, by Cyrus Karraker, where the source-trail goes dead once more.

It's no surprise at how easily these two ships were confused to be the same, given their names and those involved, but a thorough collection of primary sources of the period, presented earlier, disprove much of Rogozinski's compiled tale, which claim that Raynor bought the ship, departed Jamaica in 1689, that Kelly was elected captain in 1691 to plunder ships off the coast of Bombay, etc. Again, once compared against various period sources, the previously seemingly complete list of events is a muddied mess.

## LOCAL FOLKLORE OF THE *LOYAL JAMAICA*

Lastly, I would like to address not only the verified history that pertains to the crew of the *Loyal Jamaica*, but also the long-perpetuated local alleged claims regarding them. As I wish this book to be a complete synopsis of Raynor and the Red Sea Men of Charleston's history, and as a historian who observes folklore as well, I feel as if this book would be incomplete without including these believed tales relevant to the topic, and setting them straight here too.

By now you should have an accumulated knowledge of the events that have truly transpired and hopefully should be able to separate fact from fiction, but regardless I will follow each claim of folklore with the historical facts regarding them. Please note that these tales are essentially direct ports, entries from my other published works, in particular *Pirate Ghosts & Buried Treasures of the Southeast Coast: A Historical Assessment on Pirate Folklore.* The entries are listed by location from south to north along the coast. Also included here amid them, and not within my other aforementioned work, are the tales surrounding the location of Fenwick Hall Plantation on Johns Island.

### Seven Souls of Cap'n Sams' Spit: Kiawah Island, SC

Near Kiawah and Seabrook Island along South Carolina's coast lies an elongated stretch of land known as Captain Sam's Spit, or "Cap'n Sams" Spit. On the ocean side you'll see miles of unspoiled beach, healthy bird

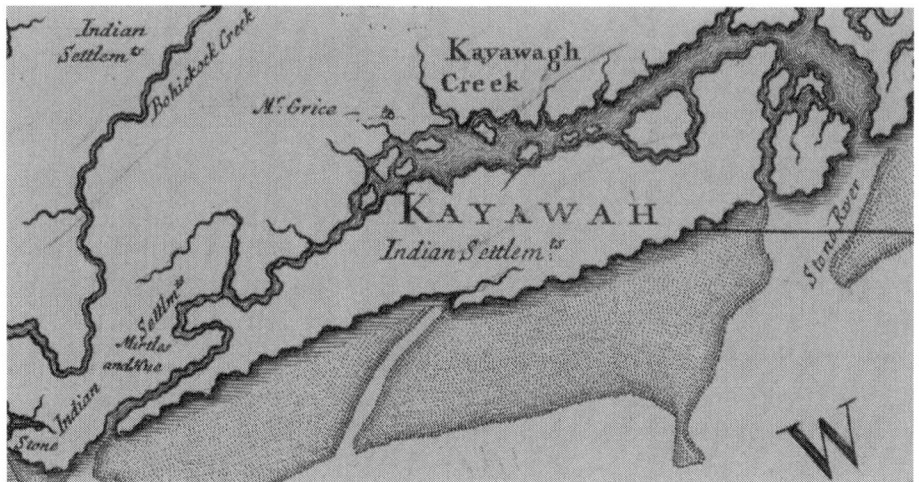

(**Figure 26**: *Cropped portion of a map of "South Carolina," circa 1689, depicting Kiawah Island, with the southern-most narrow tip being modern-day Sams Spit*)

nesting areas, and loggerhead sea turtle tracks leading from fresh nests. On the backside are dolphin strand-feeding areas. It is a fragile piece of a barrier island, long considered unstable as over the years the tides have reshaped the land. Photographs from as far back as 1974 show the stretch of land as but a sandbar, which would have been the case far back in the past of 1692.

In 1692, pirate Captain George Raynor arrived from the Red Sea, with his crew known as the Red Sea Men aboard the *Loyal Jamaica*. They moored in Seewee Bay. He and his men had made it big, and after a quick stop at the pirate haven of St. Mary's, Madagascar, they had opted to call it quits and settle down, bound for Charles Towne, South Carolina. After trials and tribulations regarding the town officials, they attained the most favorable result. Supposedly, among these men was Sams himself.

The fortune, which had been divided among Raynor's crew, immediately began going into Charles Towne's businesses as the men settled down, immensely helping the struggling colony to stay afloat economically. George Raynor would even make the purchase of the entire island of Kiawah for himself. Rumor has it however, that Sams didn't enjoy the spotlight of fame that their fortune had brought, and simply wanted to be left alone. In response to this, Raynor graciously gifted to him a small spit of land consisting of a the southern sandbar, inlet, and creek; so he could live out his days in seclusion as he wished. Local Kiawah natives would soon become friends with Sams, nicknaming the sailor "Capn' Sams" and referring to his new location as such.

Raynor's crew broke apart and went many different ways once in Charles Towne. Some would stay in the area. Some became progenitors of current-day wealthy lineages, while others of the remaining crew would leave to other locations to settle down. The story goes that seven of Raynor's men had turned too heavily to drink, and squandered their wealth, and then decided to seek out Sams to see what he had left of his cut. The scoundrels would seek out the native Kiawah in a small boat, in search of where Sams ended up, and learned that he had taken up residence on the end of Kiawah, on a beach spit of sand which often became flooded when the seas became tumultuous with storms. His land was said to be indicated by a metal post that stood even with the top of one of the dunes, with one native offering to lead them to the location. Another native however would make it to Sams first and alert him of the men searching for him. Fearing what they could possibly want, Sams would then travel across the inlet and hide, while his ex-crewmates would arrive to his abandoned shack.

When the men angrily questioned the natives about Sams' whereabouts, it had sunk in that these men from Charles Towne meant to cause harm to Sams, and so the native crafted a lie, stating that he had unfortunately passed away a week prior, falling victim to yellow fever. Unmoved by the story, the men set out with shovels from their boat to the metal post, and quickly got to work digging. About two feet down, they ran into palmetto logs, which had been used to shore up loose sand, creating a laid out square, eight-feet on each side. In the center this area, the pirates kept digging. Down and down, until around the eight-foot mark where it became impossible to throw more sand out of the hole. Still finding nothing, the pirates rowed back to the natives to acquire baskets to help them proceed.

They would note along the way, the abnormal temperature for an October, and would then arrive back at the native settlement, which was mysteriously devoid of inhabitants. Helping themselves to food left about, and taking supplies that were needed, they returned once more to the hole. The digging resumed, albeit slow and tedious, hauling the baskets out with rope, over and again. They made note that the surf seemed angry, but they set aside concern and steadily dug. At fourteen feet of depth, they believed they would be close, with the sand indicating that they were near sea level as it became damp. By this point, the sun had dipped below the horizon and the rain had begun from the storm, with the wind howling as it blew over the open pit. Before their lanterns were extinguished, they'd seen it - the glimmer of buried Turkish gold.

Then, the first wave would crash over the pit, followed by another, and more in quick succession. The walls of the hole gave way. The pirates, in their greed for treasure had dug a grave for themselves. When Sams returned the following day, he found nothing remaining of his shack, nor where the post had been. The natives would later claim that on the anniversary of the event the following year, the surf would become unusually loud, and they could hear the cries of the seven dying men coming from the spit of land. As the story goes, whenever Sams would sail up to Charles Towne, seven dolphins would cavort around his boat as he passed along his spit of land, before propelling themselves onto the beach.[10]

This entry above has been repeated here with some minor corrections from the original story, that had inconsistencies with documented facts. In the original version of the tale, it is dated 1682; ten years before Raynor's arrival to the bay, and claims the treasure Raynor arrived with was that of Spanish gold, as opposed to the Middle Eastern gains from the Red Sea that he brought to the port town. The story also claims that only seven of his crew remained in Charles Towne, who would all die on the spit of land, leaving only Sams as the sole remaining member in the area; which absolutely was not the case. It also describes the alluded hurricane that seals the pirates to their doomed fate occurring in October of 1692, and according to documentation of recorded hurricanes in that year, hurricanes occurred in Havana, Jamaica and Belize; but not in along Carolina. This isn't to say a very strong storm didn't occur or wasn't recorded though.

Most damning for the legend, is that the spit of land is in fact instead named for Captain Robert Sams, who was a colonial-era planter who lived upon Johns Island, who passed away in the year 1760.[11] With documents regarding Raynor's arrival to Charles Towne, there are no mentions of a man named Sams. While a number of people seem to know of Sams' Spit being either haunted, or being the location of pirate treasure, it seems to be a fairly new legend, that while it has spread among locals, it has only existed for about sixteen years as of 2025, and which seemingly originates from an online article on Halloween of 2009. I can find no references to this story prior to that, and it might be assumed it was the article's author, Sidi Limehouse's, own original Halloween tale.

## Treasure of Raynor's Isle: Kiawah, SC

According to folklore, Captain George Raynor was a pirate who operated from the backside of Kiawah Island near Old Dock Creek in the 17th century, who plied the waters surrounding Charles Town. One day, following a great hurricane in 1682, he and his crew struck out south and captured a large amount of gold from a Spanish vessel. Arriving back to Charles Town with plundered gold below decks, he donated generously to town officials to have them overlook his crimes at sea. As the legend goes, locals looked the other way, and Raynor was granted ownership of the entirety of Kiawah Island. It has since been rumored to be the location of where the pirate captain once buried an amount of the Spanish gold.[12]

In time, Raynor sold half of the island to a man named Captain William Davis, and following his own death, his daughter Mary inherited his remaining land. As mentioned, while based off of historical facts, Raynor never lived on Kiawah, never operated as a pirate in the waters surrounding South Carolina after his arrival, never brought in Spanish gold, and was never 'gifted' Kiawah Island. In general, this claim of treasure seems to be nothing more than a real estate company using obscure pirate history to drum up interest in Kiawah properties.

## The Legends of Fenwick Hall: Johns Island, SC

Not far off the Maybank Highway and near the Stono River is the old two-story brick plantation home of Fenwick Hall, also known as "Fenwick Castle," situated on Johns Island. The site is known to have been a prominent location dealing with pirates, and was the site of much tragedy leading to its currently haunted state. One such ghost is that of Ann Fenwick, who lived in the home in the years preceeding the Revolutionary War. Ann, in her late teens, had been secretly courting a lowly stable-boy named Tony, and when this secret came to light her father, Edward Fenwick, certainly dissapproved. Furious, her father was said to have made Tony stand atop a horse with a noose tightened around his neck leading up to the boughs of an old oak tree, and placed into his daughter's hand the riding crop to strike the horse. Ann remained distraught for the remainder of her life. After her death, those on the property are said to have reported hearing the hall filled with mournful cries, footsteps in the halls, and Ann distantly calling out for for her beloved Tony.[13]

It is even said that the famous female pirate, Ann Bonny would reside at this home for a time. She and her associates had been captured in 1720, and after her imprisonment in Spanish Town, Jamaica, she returned home to Charleston in Carolina. However, she quickly found herself in captivity once more, this time by Robert Fenwick, a notorious old pirate who had been one of Charleston's Red Sea Men. Held captive in Fenwick Hall, she served as his captive mistress, spending much of her time locked away upstairs or down in the dungeon. Robert used the house as the center of his illicit smuggling business, ferrying goods back and forth from the Stono River via secret underground tunnels on the property.[14]

(**Figure 27**: *"Fenwick Hall Plantation," photography by Historic American Buildings Survey, 1933*)

As riveting of a claim as the above is, the entirety of these allegations regarding Robert Fenwick and Bonny are fabricated. Ann Bonny, allegedly from Charles Towne, had indeed become captured in late 1720 and imprisoned in Jamaica, but despite the variety of claims of her escaping or being bailed out by her lawyer father we now have proof of Ann's ending; burial records of Spanish Town uncovered within the last decade note her burial about ten years later, interred into the same grounds as her former fellow pirate crewmate, Mary Read. Most damning of all for the tale is that, as you know from this work, that Robert Fenwick never even lived in the completed home, as he died three years before its completion.

Today, Fenwick Hall still exists, but after decades of it serving different uses, it now remains in a decrepit state. The building currently sits on private owned property and is not open to the general public for visitation.

## Buried Treasure of the Loyal Jamaica: Bulls Island, SC

As short as the statement is, for some time it was believed that upon the arrival of the Red Sea pirates to Seewee Bay, adjacent to Bulls Island, that they had taken the vast majority of their plunder ashore and hid it away on the isle - retrieving it as needed and claiming to have brought in far less than there factually was. Simply put, one local claim is that it was not retrieved by them in its entirety.

Lore among the living descendants of pirate Captain George Raynor has it that there is reason to believe that the captain had buried an amount of treasure upon Bulls Island, South Carolina, during his time living in the state during the 1690's. According to *The Rayners of Massachusetts: And Where We Came From*, a book published regarding the family lineage in 2021, it briefly states a descendant named Robert Raynor discovered an old map with an 'X' marked onto Bulls Island, South Carolina, along with directions that provided distances in paces, and notable landmarks. However, nothing ever came of it.[15]

It would seem that something had been mistaken during the writing of the aforementioned book after having spoken myself with descendant Robert Raynor of South Carolina. First, as Robert was already aware, they, like many before them, had conflated the two pirate Raynors. Robert Raynor of South Carolina is actually a descendant of Josiah Raynor of New England, and had relocated down south - and the map was but one of multiple that were created by Robert himself in modern times, meant for his young grandchildren to follow as a fun pirate

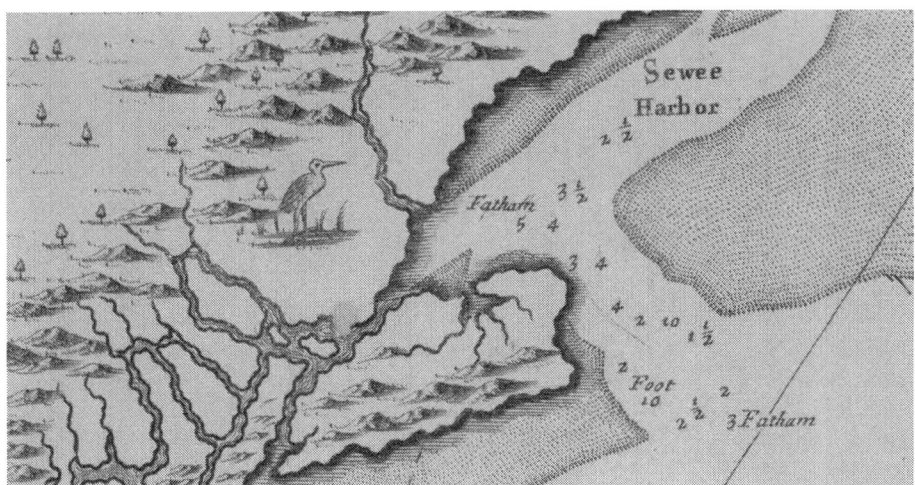

(**Figure 28**: *Cropped portion of a map of "South Carolina," circa 1689, depicting the large Bulls Island on the southern side of the Seewee Harbor*)

treasure hunt activity regarding their lineage, that of Josiah. Confusingly for the Rayners of New England, Robert here in South Carolina had taken up to boating the coasts, and both freqented and published a book about Bulls Island - the same island George Raynor had once gone ashore upon arrival.[16]

While this alleged treasure map was indeed a fabrication, and the Rayners of Massachusetts had mistaken George for Josiah as a result of the confusion over Robert, who's not to say there isn't something still remaining out on Bulls Island, unintentially lost long ago by the "privateers," perhaps even a piece of Arabian gold...

(**Figure 29**: *"Bulls Island Eastern Shore, Boneyard Beach," photography by Adam Morrow, 2020*)

# EPILOGUE

Thus concludes an overlooked yet important part of history that needed to be told - the full and concise, true tale of Raynor's Red Sea pirates of the *Loyal Jamaica*, and how Arabian gold played a pivotal role in contributing to the bustling port city that Charleston became. At best the tale of George Raynor and his men often only served as minor footnotes within pirate history books when addressing the Pirate Round and Red Sea Piracy regarding Henry Every and Thomas Tew. Alternatively they are brought up only briefly when regarded by local sources. Their names may not exist on plaques, or be featured at any historic sites around Charleston, but these people mattered. What they did mattered. Their descendants became some of the biggest names that we still speak frequently today in South Carolina's lowcountry, and their story deserved to be told in full. In Charleston, we literally walk among the foundations that pirates helped build.

Thank you for your interest, and for those of you who have supported my prior works as well, I can't thank you all enough. Assembling and publishing this book has been a long time coming, and was something I really wanted to exist, as so many sources conflated numerous things, and operated off of supposition. While my future books will likely explore more distant regions when addressing pirates, I share this, as an author and historian, to be my meaningful contribution to Charleston's history.

- Captain Marrow

# SOURCES

## Chapter One

[1] National Army Museum, *Nine Years War*. nam.ac.uk, Accessed February 10, 2025

[2] Kemp, Peter C. L., *Brethren of the Coast: The British and French Buccaneers of the South Sea*. Florida, Krieger Publishing Company, 1961

[3] J.W. Fortescue, *Calendar of State Papers, Colonial Series, America and West Indies, 1689-1692*. London: His Majesty's Stationary Office, 1901

[4] idem

[5] Letter by Jean Prairier, Cape Town, March 30, 1690 in Debian, Gabriel & Marcel Delafosse, *Revue Francaise d'Histoire d'outre-mer*. 1961

[6] Salley, Alexander S., "The Deposition of Henry Perry, Thomas Pinckney, Edmund Medlicott, and George Raynor, Charlestown, 22 August/1 September," from "Abstracts from the Records of the Court of Ordinary of the Province of South Carolina" in *Journal of the Grand Council of South Carolina: April 11, 1692 - September 26, 1692*. The Historical Commission of South Carolina, by the Suite Company, Columbia, S.C., 1907

Also, *The South Carolina Historical and Geneological Magazine, Vol. 8, No. 4*. October, 1907

[7] Kelly, James, "*A Full and True Discovery of all the Robberies, Pyracies, and other Notorious Actions, of that Famous English Pyrate, Capt. James Kelly.*" July, 1700

[8] *AGI Santo Domingo/111/R.1/N.8*, Letter from Governor Severino de Manzaneda to the King of Spain, August 11, 1691.

[9] Millar, John F. "*Buccaneers Davis, Wafer & Hingson, and the Ship Batchelor's Delight.*" 2010

[10] *CSPCS 1689-1692, No. 1104*, 1692 - As noted by scholar Reynald Laprise, no names of ships nor captains are given.

*Sources*

# Chapter Two

[1] *"Canarian-American Trade in the 18th Century (Part 1)."* canariasCNNews.com, July 7, 2018

[2] Kelly, James, *"A Full and True Discovery of all the Robberies, Pyracies, and other Notorious Actions, of that Famous English Pyrate, Capt. James Kelly."* July, 1700

[3] Rogozinski, Jan, *"Pirates!: Brigands, Buccaneers, and Privateers in Fact, Fiction, and Legend."* Facts on File, 1995

[4] Grey, Charles, *"Pirates of the Eastern Seas (1618-1723): A Lurid Page of History."* London: S. Low, Marston & co., ltd, 1933

[5] Frick, Matthew, *A Gold Chain, A Wooden Leg, and a Treasure Chest.* 2021

[6] Richards, John F., *The Mughal Empire.* Cambridge University Press, 2012

[7] Dasgupta, K., *"How Learned Were the Mughals: Reflections on Muslim Libraries in India."* The Journal Library of History, 1975

[8] Werner, Louis "Mughal Maal" in *Saudi Aramco World, Volume 62, Number 4.* July/August, 2011

[9] Hansen, Eric, "Pashmina: Kashmir's Best Cashmere" in *Saudi Aramco World, Volume 62, Number 4.* July/August, 2002

[10] Vaia, *Mughal Trade*, vaia.com/themughalempire, accessed February 10, 2025

[11] idem

[12] idem

[13] Millar, Simon, *Vienna 1683: Christian Europe Repels the Ottomans.* Osprey, 2008

[14] Nadri, Ghulam Ahmad, "Merchants in the Late Mughal Gujarat: Evidence from Two Major Persian Sources" in *Proceedings of the Indian History Congress, Vol. 58.* 1997

[15] Hariram K., & Krishna Murthy, replies to *"What Was the Value of 1 Rupee in Terms of the US Dollar During Aurangzeb's Rule?"* quora.com, 2021

[16] "BP Pauses all Red Sea Shipments After Rebel Attacks" in *BBC News*, December 18, 2023

[17] "Egypt's Suez Canal Blocked by Huge Container Ship" in *BBC News* - March 23, 2021

[18] Dodwell, Henry, *Records of Fort St. George: Diary and Consultation Book of 1691.* Madras: Government Press, 1917

[19]Orvington, J., *A Voyage to Surratt in the Year 1689 Giving a Large Account of That City and It's Inhabitants and of the English Factory There.* Londres: Jacob Tonson, 1696

[20]Martineau, Alfred, *Memoires de Francois Martin, Fondateur de Pondichery, 1665-1696, Vol. III.* Paris: Societe de l'histoire des Colonies Francaises, 1694

[21]Dodwell, Henry, *Records of Fort St. George: Diary and Consultation Book of 1691.* Madras: Government Press, 1917

# Chapter Three

[1]Baker, C.A. Jr., *Chapter 30 - The Pirate Adam Baldridge.* bakerfamilytree.blogspot.com, January 26, 2012

[2]'Idylle Beach, "History and Myths" in *History on Ile Sainte-Marie.* idyllebeach.com, N/D

[3]Vallar, Cindy, *A Pirate Lexicon.* cindyvallar.com, 2012

[4]*TNS CO 5/104/No. 30, Deposition of Adam Baldridge*, New York, 5/15 May, 1699

[5]Natural World Safaris, *Ile Sainte Marie.* naturalworldsafaris.com/africa/madagascar, N/D

[6]*TNS CO 5/104/No. 30, Deposition of Adam Baldridge*, New York, 5/15 May, 1699

[7]"Privateering One Day, Pirating the Next" in *Post and Courier.* 2014

[8]*Seth Sothel, Governor of Albemarle 1682 to 1689, Governor of "Ye Lands South and West of Cape Feare" 1690 to 1692.* carolina.com/carolina/governors

[9]Salley, Alexander S., "The Deposition of Peter Skroder A Dane by Nation aged Twenty Four Years or Thereabouts Taken this Twentyeth Day of Aprill 1692" in *Journal of the Grand Council of South Carolina: April 11, 1692 - September 26, 1692.* The Historical Commission of South Carolina, by the Suite Company, Columbia, S.C., 1907

[10]UK Overseas Territories Team, *Ascension Island.* brahmsonline.kew.org, 2025

[11]Mills, Alan P., *Capturing the Diversity - Dampier's Drip.* alanpmills.wordpress.com, May 18, 2016

[12]Salley, Alexander S., "The Deposition of Peter Skroder A Dane by Nation aged Twenty Four Years or Thereabouts Taken this

*Sources*

Twentyeth Day of Aprill 1692" in *Journal of the Grand Council of South Carolina: April 11, 1692 - September 26, 1692*. The Historical Commission of South Carolina, by the Suite Company, Columbia, S.C., 1907
[13] idem

# Chapter Four

[1] Salley, Alexander S., *Journal of the Grand Council of South Carolina: April 11, 1692 - September 26, 1692*. The Historical Commission of South Carolina, by the Suite Company, Columbia, S.C., 1907
[2] idem
[3] idem
[4] idem
[5] idem
[6] idem
[7] idem
[8] Edgar, Walter B. and N. Louise Bailey, *Biographical Directory of the South Carolina House of Representatives, Volume II: the Commons House of Assembly 1692-1775.* 1977
"John Alexander: Biography." wikitree.com/alexander-2238
[9] Roper, L.H., "Johnson, Sir Nathaniel" in *South Carolina Encyclopedia*. University of South Carolina, Institute for Southern Studies. June 8, 2016
[10] Roper, L.H., "Moore, James, Sr." in *South Carolina Encyclopedia*. University of South Carolina, Institute for Southern Studies. June 8, 2016
[11] Trinkley, Michael and Debi Hacker, *Schoolbred's Old Settlement: Excavations at 38CH123, Kiawah Island, Charleston County, South Carolina: Research Series 70*. Chicora Foundation, Inc, December 2009
[12] Holmes, Henry S., "Robert Gibbes, Governor of South Carolina, and Some of His Descendants" in *The South Carolina Historical and Genealogical Magazine*. 1911
[13] Lewis, J.D., *Landgrave - Edmund Bellinger, Sr.*. carolana.com/nobility, 2021
[14] Palmer, Claire, Joseph Palmer, *1690s Pirate, Who Knew Capt. Kidd*. genealogy.com, July 25, 2004
[15] Kehoe, Mark C., *"The History of Sea and Pirate Surgeons, Page 10."* piratesurgeon.com, accessed February 13, 2025

[16] Vallar, Cindy, *"Stede Bonnet (Continued)."* cindyvallar.com/sbonnet., accessed February 13, 2025

[17] Salley, Alexander S. *The South Carolina Historical and Genealogical Magazine, Vol. 8, No. 4, Abstracts from the Records of the Court of Ordinary of the Province of South Carolina, 1692-1670.* 1907

[18] McCrady, Edward, *The History of South Carolina Under The Proprietary Government 1670-1719.* The Macmillan Company, 1897

[19] "1692: Earthquake destroys Jamaican Town" in *This Day in History.* history.com, date accessed February 12, 2025

[20] Salley, Alexander S., *Journal of the Grand Council of South Carolina: April 11, 1692 - September 26, 1692.* The Historical Commission of South Carolina, by the Suite Company, Columbia, S.C., 1907

[21] Marley, David F. *Pirates of the Americas Vol. 1 & 2.* ABC-CLIO, LCC, 2010

[22] Salley, Alexander S., *Journal of the Grand Council of South Carolina: April 11, 1692 - September 26, 1692.* The Historical Commission of South Carolina, by the Suite Company, Columbia, S.C., 1907

[23] Salley, Alexander S. *The South Carolina Historical and Genealogical Magazine, Vol. 8, No. 4, Abstracts from the Records of the Court of Ordinary of the Province of South Carolina, 1692-1670.* 1907

[24] idem

[25] idem

[26] *Jonathan Amory (1654-1699): Speaker of the Assembly of South Carolina, etc.* americanaristocracy.com, Accessed February 16, 2025

[27] *Tenth Generation: 716. Jonathan Amory.* msa.maryland.gov, Accessed February 16, 2025

[28] *TNS CO 5/104/No. 30, Deposition of Adam Baldridge*, New York, May, 1699

[29] Hewatt, Alexander, *An Historical Account of the Rise and Progress of The Colonies of South Carolina and Georgia, Volume 1.* 1829

[30] Green, Jack P., "A Letter From South Carolina" by Thomas Nairne in *Selling a New World: Two Colonial South Carolina Pamphlets.* University of South Carolina, 1989

[31] idem

[32] Nettels, Curtis P., *The Money Supply of the American Colonies Before 1720.* Madison, Wis, 1934

[33] *Charleston Collects: South Asian Art.* gibbesmuseum.org, Accessed February 16, 2025

*Sources*

[34]Salley, Alexander S. *The South Carolina Historical and Genealogical Magazine, Vol. 8, No. 4, Abstracts from the Records of the Court of Ordinary of the Province of South Carolina, 1692-1670.* 1907

# Chapter Five

[1]Salley, Alexander S., *The South Carolina Historical And Genealogical Magazine, Vol. 8, No. 3.* 1907
[2]idem
[3]idem
[4]*Daniel Horry (abt. 1662 - 1696).* wikitree.com/horry-31, accessed February 13, 2025
[5]Edwards, Kieth, *Daniel Horry: 1662-1696.* findagrave.com, May 17, 2012, Accessed February 14, 2025
[6]Gannett, Henry, *The Origin of Certain Place Names in the United States.* 1907
[7]Maryland Council, *Proceedings of the Council of Maryland, 1636-1770, Volume 23.* Baltimore, Maryland Historical Society, 1903
[8]idem
[9]Saunders, William Laurence, Walter Clark, and Stephen Beauregard Weeks, The *State Records of North Carolina: Volume 1.* Nash Brothers, University of Michigan. 1886
[10]*Thomas Tew.* www.jcs-group.com. Accessed February 14, 2025
[11]Hollingsworth, Bill, *Thomas Hollingsworth - Pirate or Privateer?* January, 2009
[12]Rogozinski, Jan, *Honor Among Thieves: Captain Kidd, Henry Avery, and the Pirate Democracy in the Indian Ocean.* Mechanicsburg, PA: Stackpole Books, 2000
[13]Little, Bennerson, *How a Mystery Pirate Captain Gave Us Rafael Sabatini's Captain Blood & the Films of Errol Flynn.* bennersonlittle.com, November 23, 2021, Accessed February 14, 2025
[14]Hauser, John R., "1701" in *Fenwick Hall Short Stories: True Stories Surrounding Those That Lived at Fenwick and Their Families… John's Island, SC.* fenwickhall.com, Accessed February 19, 2025
[15]Charleston County, *Building Fenwick Hall.* storyoffenwickhall.com, Accessed February 15, 2025

[16] Weber, Mabel L., "The Thomas Pinckney Family of South Carolina" in *The South Carolina Historical and Genealogical Magazine, Vol. 39, No. 1*. South Carolina Historical Society, January, 1938

[17] Southwick, Leslie, *Presidential Also-Rans and Running Mates, 1788 through 1996*. McFarland, 1998

[18] *Privateering One Day, Pirating the Next*. postandcourier.com, November 3, 2014, Accessed February 20, 2025

[19] *Dorcas Davis (1675 - 1715)*. ancestry.com/records/dorcas-davis, Accessed February 13, 2025

[20] Hallen, A.W. Cornelius, *The Registers of St. Botolph, Bishopgate, London, Vol. III*. 1895

[21] Bannerman, Bruce W., *The Registers of St. Helen's, Bishopgate, London*. London, 1904

[22] Scott, Merilee, *George Raynor: -1688*.findagrave.com, Accessed February 13, 2025

[23] Widder, Agnes Haigh, "Daniel Defoe in Brief. His Writings. And Plague" in *Defoe and the Plague in London, 1664-1665*. Michigan State University Libraries, accessed February 13, 2025

[24] *The Great Fire of London*. london-fire.gov.uk, accessed February 13, 2025

[25] Salley, Alexander S. and Olsberg, *Records of the Court of Ordinary of the Province of South Carolina 1692-1700*. 1973

[26] *Dorcas Davis (1675 - 1715)*. ancestry.com/records/dorcas-davis, Accessed February 13, 2025

[27] Butler, Nic Ph.D, *Planning Charleston's First "Fortress," 1695-1696*. ccpl.org, Accessed February 14, 2025

[28] Butler, Nic Ph.D, *Charleston's Half-Moon Battery, 1694-1768*. ccpl.org, August 13, 2021, Accessed February 14, 2025

[29] Mears, Neal F., *A History of the Heverly Family, Including the Spellings of Hever, Heverle, Heverley, Everle, Everley, Everleigh, Eveleigh, Everlegh, Everly, Everly, and Eveleth*.The Bates Printing Co., 1945

[30] Salley, Alexander S. and Olsberg, *Records of the Court of Ordinary of the Province of South Carolina 1692-1700*. 1973

[31] idem

[32] Mayor Orban, Steve, "Special Presentation of Kiawah Land Grant Deed" in *The Island Connection, Vol. 4, Issue 20*. January 21, 2011

[33] South Carolina, Probate Court, *South Carolina Will and Related Probate Matters, Land and Property Records, Public Records, Some Marriage Contracts, 171, 1692-1868*. Probate Court

## Sources

(Charleston County). 18 microfilm reels; 35mm, Filmed by the Genealogical Society of Utah, 1959. Will Book directory pg.311, Will Book pg.222

[34] Trinkley, Michael, *The History and Archaeology of Kiawah Island, Charleston County, South Carolina: Research Series 30.* Chicora Foundation, Inc., 1993

[35] *McGing Lines (Person Page 846).* mcging.org, accessed February 27, 2025

[36] Salley Alexander S., *Journal of the Commons House of Assembly of South Carolina For the Session Beginning January 30, 1696, and Ending March 17, 1696.* Columbia: The State Company for the Historical Commission of South Carolina, 1908

[37] Payne, Laura, *Kiawah Island.* brittanica.com/place/kiawah-island, Accessed February 14, 2025

[38] Sirmans, M. Eugene. *Colonial South Carolina: A Political History: 1663-1763.* University of North Carolina Press, Chapel Hill. 1966

[39] Hughson, Shirley C., *The Carolina Pirates and Colonial Commerce, 1670-1740.* John Hopkins University Studies in Historical and Political Science, Twelfth Series, 1894

[40] idem

[41] *Records of the Court of Ordinary of the Province of South Carolina 1692-1700*: Vol. 1

[42] Hughson, Shirley C., *The Carolina Pirates and Colonial Commerce, 1670-1740.* John Hopkins University Studies in Historical and Political Science, Twelfth Series, 1894

[43] Hirsch, Arthur Henry, *The Huguenots of Colonial South Carolina.* Durham, North Carolina, Duke University Press, 1928

[44] Hughson, Shirley C., *The Carolina Pirates and Colonial Commerce, 1670-1740.* John Hopkins University Studies in Historical and Political Science, Twelfth Series, 1894

[45] Fortescue, J.W., "A Paper Submitted to the Commisioners of Customs by Edward Randolph, America and West Indies: August 1696, 17-31," in *Calendar of State Papers - America and West Indies: Volume 15, 1696-1697.* London, His Majesty's Stationary Office, 1904

[46] Preservation Society of Charleston, *1700 (September 3) Cyclone.* halseymap.com, Accessed February 19, 2025

[47] Salley, Alexander, "The Present State of Affairs in Carolina, by John Ash, 1706" in *Narratives of Early Carolina 1650-1708.* New York, 1911

[48] Lee, Robert E. *Blackbeard the Pirate*. John F. Blair, 1974
[49] Woodard, Colin, *The Republic of Pirates: Being the True and Surprising Story of the Caribbean Pirates and the Man Who Brought Them Down*. New York, Harcourt, 2007

# Chapter Six

[1] *Geneanet Community Trees Index: Josiah Raynor*. ancestry.com, 2022, Accessed February 14, 2025
[2] Torrey, Clarence Almon, *New England Marriages: Prior to 1700*. Genealogical Publishing Co.; Baltimore, MD, USA, 1985
[3] *Geneanet Community Trees Index: Uriah Raynor*. Ancestry.com, Accessed February 14, 2025
[4] Jameson, John Franklin, *Privateering and Piracy in the Colonial Period*. York: Macmillan, 1923
[5] *The Raynor/Rayner Family of Long Island*. longislandgeneology.com, Accessed February 20, 2025
Also, *Josiah Raynor*. geni.com, Accessed February 20, 2025
[6] Kelly, James, "*A Full and True Discovery of all the Robberies, Pyracies, and other Notorious Actions, of that Famous English Pyrate, Capt. James Kelly*." July, 1700
[7] Willard Hallam, Bonner, "The Ballad of Captain Kidd" in *American Literature: Vol. 15, No. 9*. Duke University Press, 1944
[8] Burney, James, *History of the Buccaneers of America*. London, Printed by L. Hansard & Sons, for Payne and Foss, 1816
[9] Harbury, Katharine E., "Edward Davis (d. after 10 March 1692)," in *Dictionary of Virginia Biography*. Library of Virginia, 1998
[10] Limehouse, Sidi, *The Seven Pirate Ghosts of Capn Sams*. islandconnectionnews.com, October 31, 2009
Also, Marrow, Captain, *Pirate Ghosts & Buried Treasures of the Southeast Coast: A Historical Assessement on Pirate Folklore*. Picaroon Press, 2023
[11] Association Voice, *Captain Sams Inlet FAQ*. associationvoice.com, Accessed June 10, 2021
Also, Sams Bond, Lula, and Laura Sams Sanders, *The South Carolina Historical Magazine Vol. 64, No. 1*. South Carolina Historical Society, 1963

*Sources*

[12]Harrington, Pam, *A History of Kiawah Island.* pamharringtonexclusives.com, Accessed June 10, 2021
Also, Marrow, Captain, *Pirate Ghosts & Buried Treasures of the Southeast Coast: A Historical Assessement on Pirate Folklore.* Picaroon Press, 2023

[13]Butler, Margaret Rhett, "The Legend of Fenwick Castle" in *Charleston County Stories & Legends.* geocities.com, July 29, 2004, Accessed February 19, 2025

[14]Miles, Suzannah Smith, "Lowcountry Stories You've Never Heard" in *Charleston Living Magazine, Jan-Feb.* 2018

[15]Rayner, Edward, *The Rayners of Massachusetts: And Where We Came From.* Edward Rayner, 2021

[16]Raynor, Robert, *Pirate Treasure.* raynoronthecoast.com, January 12, 2015, Accessed August 12, 2021
Also, Raynor, Robert, *Treasure of Bulls Island.* Interview. Conducted by Adam Morrow, May 2023

*Arabian Gold: Charleston's Red Sea Pirates of* 1692

*List of Figures*

# LIST OF FIGURES

All images used in this work are believed to be in the public domain.

**Opening Art:** "A Frigate at Sea," by Pierre Puget, 17th century. https://commons.wikimedia.org/wiki/File:A_Frigate_at_Sea_MET_DP807953.jpg, CC-Zero

**Figure 1. Source:** "Map Showing the Harbours of Port Royal and Kingston, Jamaica," by Edward Long, 1774. This image is part of the Public Domain, and was retrieved at Wikimedia Commons, https://commons.wikimedia.org/wiki/File:Map_showing_the_harbours_of_Port_Royal_and_Kingston,_Jamaica_Wellcome_L0063041.jpg, https://creativecommons.org/licenses/by/4.0/deed.en

**Figure 2. Source:** "View of Port Royal and Kingston Harbours," by Edward Long, 1774. This image is part of the Public Domain, and was retrieved at Wikimedia Commons, https://commons.wikimedia.org/wiki/File:Map_showing_the_harbours_of_Port_Royal_and_Kingston,_Jamaica_Wellcome_L0063041.jpg, https://creativecommons.org/licenses/by/4.0/deed.en

**Figure 3. Source:** "Vue de la ville du Port de Paix," by Nicolas Ponce & Nicolas Ozanne, 1791. This image is part of the Public Domain, and was retrieved at Wikimedia Commons, https://commons.wikimedia.org/wiki/File:Vue_de_la_ville_du_Port_de_Paix_(Nicolas_Ozanne_et_Nicolas_Ponce).jpg, CC-PD-Mark,

**Figure 4. Source:** "Map of the Cape Verde Islands, 1683," by Alain Manesson Mallet. This image is part of the Public Domain, and was retrieved at Wikimedia Commons, https://commons.wikimedia.org/wiki/File:Map_of_the_Cape_Verde_Islands,_1683.jpg, CC-PD-Mark,

**Figure 5. Source:** "Henry Every," 18th century engraving. This image is part of the Public Domain, and was retrieved at Wikimedia Commons, https://commons.wikimedia.org/wiki/File:Henry_Every.gif, CC-PD-Mark, PD-Art (PD-old-100)

**Figure 6. Source:** Cropped portion of "Aurangzeb, Grand Moghol," by Nicolas de Larmessin, 1690. This image is part of the Public Domain, and was retrieved at Wikimedia Commons, https://commons.wikimedia.org/wiki/File:Estampes_par_Nicolas_d

e_Larmessin.f153.Aurangzeb,_grand_moghol_(cropped).jpg, CC-PD-Mark

**Figure 7.** Source: "Silver Rupee of Aurangzeb," private collection, 17th century. This image is part of the Public Domain, and was retrieved at Wikimedia Commons, https://commons.wikimedia.org/wiki/File:Silver_Rupee_of_Aurangazeb_AH1096.jpg, CC-BY-SA-3.0, private collection of Drnsreedhar1959, photographed November 21, 2010

**Figure 8.** Source: "Captain Tew Attacks the Ship From India," Unknown artist, 1837. Depicted in "The Pirates Own Book," by Charles Ellms. This image is part of the Public Domain, and was retrieved at Wikimedia Commons, https://commons.wikimedia.org/wiki/File:Captain_Tew_attacks_the_ship_from_India.jpg, CC-PD-Mark

**Figure 9.** Source: "Map of Madagascar, 1685," by Alain Manesson Mallet. This image is part of the Public Domain, and was retrieved at Wikimedia Commons, https://commons.wikimedia.org/wiki/File:Map_of_Madagascar,_1685.jpg, CC-PD-Mark, PD Old

**Figure 10.** Source: "Sainte Marie Island - Madagascar, 1601," by Etienne de Flacourt. This image is part of the Public Domain, and was retrieved at Wikimedia Commons, https://commons.wikimedia.org/wiki/File:Sainte_Marie_Island-Madagascar-1601.jpg, CC-PD-Mark, PD-old-70-expired

**Figure 11.** Source: "Capt. George Lowther and his Company at Port May in the Gulph of Matique," 1730s. This image is part of the Public Domain, and was retrieved at Wikimedia Commons, https://commons.wikimedia.org/wiki/File:Capt._George_Lowther_and_hiscompany_at_Port_Mayo_in_the_Gulph_of_Matique_LCCN2007677059.jpg, CC-PD-Mark, PD-old-100-expired

**Figure 12.** Source: "View of Fort Dauphin (Madagascar), 1685," by Alain Manesson Mallet. This image is part of the Public Domain, and was retrieved at Wikimedia Commons, https://commons.wikimedia.org/wiki/File:ViewofFortDauphin(Madagascar),1685.jpg, CC-PD-Mark, PD Old

**Figure 13.** Source: "Fernando de Noronha," photography by Cassinha Magalhaes. This image is part of the Public Domain, and was retrieved at Wikimedia Commons, https://commons.wikimedia.org/wiki/File:NORONHA_-_VISTA_MIRANTE.jpg, CC-BY-SA-4.

*List of Figures*

**Figure 14. Source:** "A Plan of the Town, Bar, Harbour and environs, of Charlestown in South Carolina..., 1780," by William Faden. This image is part of the Public Domain, and was retrieved at Wikimedia Commons, https://commons.wikimedia.org/wiki/File:A_plan_of_the_town,_bar,_harbour_and_environs,_of_Charlestown_in_South_Carolina,_with_all_the_channels,_soundings,_sailingmarks_%26c._From_the_surveys_made_in_the_colony;_engraved_by_William_Faden,_Charing_Cross,_1780._RMG_F0163.tiff, CC-PD-Mark, PD-old-100-expired, PD-Art (PD-old-100-expired)

**Figure 15. Source:** "Portrait believed to be of governor Philip Ludwell," Unknown artist. This image is part of the Public Domain, and was retrieved at Wikimedia Commons, https://commons.wikimedia.org/wiki/File:PhilipLudwell.jpg, CC-PD-Mark, PD-old-70-expired

**Figure 16. Source:** "Engraving of an old portrait of Parliamentarian and colonial governor Nathaniel Johnson, 1644-1713," Unknown artist. This image is part of the Public Domain, and was retrieved at Wikimedia Commons, https://commons.wikimedia.org/wiki/File:NathanielJohnson.jpg, 1919, PD US

**Figure 17. Source:** "Port Royal Earthquake of 1692," by Jan Luyken and Pieter van der Aa. This image is part of the Public Domain, and was retrieved at Wikimedia Commons, https://commons.wikimedia.org/wiki/File:Port_Royal_earthquake_1692byJanLuykenandPietervanderAa.jpg, CC-PD-Mark, PD Old

**Figure 18. Source:** "Peter Horry Canvas Painting," late 18th century. This image is part of the Public Domain, and was retrieved at Wikimedia Commons, https://commons.wikimedia.org/wiki/File:Horry-painting-canvas-large.webp, CC-PD-Mark, PD-old-70-expired

**Figure 19. Source:** "Fenwick Hall Plantation, Johns Island, Charleston County, South Carolina," photography by Historic American Buildings Survey, 1933. This image is part of the Public Domain, and was retrieved at Wikimedia Commons, https://commons.wikimedia.org/wiki/File:Fenwick_Hall_Plantation,_Northeast_intersection_of_River_Road_%26_Maybank_Highway,_Johns_Island_(Charleston_County,_South_Carolina).jpg, PD US NPS

**Figure 20. Source:** "General Charles Cotesworth Pinckney, 1796," by James Earl. This image is part of the Public Domain, and was retrieved at Wikimedia Commons, https://commons.wikimedia.org/wiki/File:James_Earl_-GeneralCharlesCotesworthPinckney-GoogleArtProject.jpg, CC-PD- Mark, PD-old-100-expired, PD-Art (PD-old-100-expired)

**Figure 21. Source:** "The Thames in the 17th Century," which depicts a view of the river looking in the direction toward Southwark Cathedral, photography by Duncan Harris, 2012. This image is part of the Public Domain, and was retrieved at Wikimedia Commons, https://commons.wikimedia.org/wiki/File:Flickr-Duncan~_-TheThamesinthe17thCentury.jpg, CC-BY-2.0

**Figure 22. Source:** "Crisp Map of Charleston in 1711." This image is part of the Public Domain, and was retrieved at Wikimedia Commons, https://commons.wikimedia.org/wiki/File:Crisp_Map_of_Charlestonin1711.png, PD US expired

**Figure 23. Source:** "Cropped George Rainer Entry in directory, and accompanied Raynor will, Entry 53" in the "South Carolina, U.S., Wills and Probate Records, 1670-1980"

**Figure 24. Source:** "Kiawah Island, SC, USA," photography by 'olekinderhook,' 2016. This image is part of the Public Domain, and was retrieved at Wikimedia Commons, https://commons.wikimedia.org/wiki/File:Kiawah_Island,_SC,_USA-panoramio-olekinderhook(3).jpg, CC-BY-3.0

**Figure 25. Source:** Thomas Tew Chest, St. Augustine Pirate & Treasure Museum," photography by Adam Morrow, 2021. Own image.

**Figure 26. Source:** Map of "South Carolina," circa 1689. This image is part of the Public Domain, and was retrieved at Wikimedia Commons, https://commons.wikimedia.org/wiki/File:South_Carolina-btv1b85960331.jpg, Cropped, PD-old missing SDC copyright status, CC-PD-Mark, PD Old (assumed), PD US expired

**Figure 27. Source:** "Fenwick Hall Plantation," photography by Historic American Buildings Survey, 1933. This image is part of the Public Domain, and was retrieved at Wikimedia Commons, https://commons.wikimedia.org/wiki/File:Fenwick_Hall_Plantation,_Northeast_of_intersection_of_River_Road_and_Maybank_Highway,_Johns_Island,_Charleston_County,_SC_HABS_SC,10-CHAR,413-12.tif, PD US NPS

*List of Figures*

**Figure 28. Source:** Map of "South Carolina," circa 1689. This image is part of the Public Domain, and was retrieved at Wikimedia Commons, https://commons.wikimedia.org/wiki/File:South_Carolina_-_btv1b85960331.jpg, Cropped, PD-old missing SDC copyright status, CC-PD-Mark, PD Old (assumed), PD US expired

**Figure 29. Source:** "Bulls Island Eastern Shore, Boneyard Beach," Photography by Adam Morrow, 2020. Own image.

**Author Bio Picture (Interior):** "Captain Marrow at the Colonial Quarter, St. Augustine, Florida" by Warren Clinton Burdines Jr., Dos Almas Media, 2022, Used with Permission.

*Arabian Gold: Charleston's Red Sea Pirates of* 1692

# INDEX

## A

Abram, Richard
56, 58, 69
Afghanistan
27
Africa
18, 22, 25, 27, 29, 37, 49, 91,
Akbar
28
America
24, 25, 27, 40, 45, 51, 79, 84, 86
*Amity*
26, 72, 88
Amory, Jonathan
65
Arabia
27
Arundell County
71
Ashepoo
61, 74
Aurangzeb
2, 27, 28, 30, 34, 35
Austen, George
16
Ayer's Point
76

## B

Bab-el Mandeb Strait
31

*Bachelor's Delight*
13, 19, 21-23, 24-26, 31-34, 36, 40, 42, 44, 46, 48, 49, 50, 65, 87, 89-92
Bahamas
67, 72
Baldridge, Adam
16, 32, 34, 35, 39–46, 62, 65–67, 86, 91
Ballough, William
76
Bangladesh
27
Barbados
61, 65
Barlycorne, Nicholas
58
Basden, Charles
58
*Batchelor's Delight*
7, 21, 22, 26, 91, 92
Baugh, Andrew
58
Bedon, Grace
74
Bellamy, Samuel
86
Bellinger, Edmund
58, 60, 78
Bellomont, Lord
42
Bengal
27
Benier
28
Bermuda
26, 51, 72

Bishopsgate
  76, 87
Blackbeard
  11, 16, 44, 86
Blackmore, John
  71
Blanchard, Francis
  46, 58
Bombay
  93
Bonnet, Stede
  11, 61, 86
Bonny, Ann
  97, 98
Boone, John
  59, 63, 73, 74
Boston
  13, 25
Bradley, Daniel
  53
Bradley, William
  58
Brazilwood
  50
Breakneck Valley
  49
Brethren of the Coast
  14
Bulls Island
  55, 99, 100, 111, 116
Burnham, Chas
  58

# C
Calicut
  29, 36
Canary Islands
  22, 23, 89

Carolina
  7, 45, 46, 48, 50, 51, 53–57,
  60–76, 80–84, 89, 91, 94
  96–100
Clare, Roger
  58
Copley, Colonel
  71
Cotesworth
  74, 75, 115
Cotter, William
  71
Crossbye, William
  58

# D
Dampier, William
  18, 26, 49, 91
Dane
  34, 49, 62
Davis, Dorcas
  76, 78, 80, 88, 92
Davis, Edward
  18, 21, 22, , 91, 92, 97
Defoe, Daniel
  25, 108
Dewees Island
  55
Direckson, Cent
  48, 49
Dorrell
  76

# E
Edisto Island
  70
*Elizabeth*
  69, 70

*Index*

Elizabeth, Fanton Garnier
70
Eveleight, Elizabeth
81
Eveleigh, Samuel
79, 81
Every, Henry
21, 34, 72

# F

Fenwick, Robert
58, 59, 64, 73, 74, 93, 97, 98
Fernando de Noronha
50, 62, 114
Fletcher, Benjamin
40, 88
Fort Dauphin
25, 38, 39, 45–48, 62
France
13, 15–17, 25, 28, 29, 39, 44, 64, 70, 78

# G

Glaze, Gabriel
78
*Ganj-i-Sawai*
34, 72
Ghafur, Abdul
30-32, 34, 35, 62
Ghana
24
Gillchriste, James
58, 59
Gilliam, James
18
Graaf, Laurens de
15, 16
Grammont, Michel de
72

Grimball, Paul
68, 70
Gulf of Aden
24, 29–32, 62
Guppell, John
58

# H

Haiti
13
Half-Moon Battery
78, 79, 108
Haminett, Thomas
80
Harrison, Thomas
16–19, 22, 48, 64, 68, 89
Havana
22, 96
Stillery, Henry
58
Holloway, Henry
63
Petty, Henry
64
Hobart, Josiah
88
Hornigold, Benjamin
85
Horry, Daniel
46, 61, 70
Horry, Peter
70
Hyrne, Edward
85

# I

Inchequin, Lord
71, 71

121

India
    27–29, 31–33, 35
Isaac, Massique
    58

## J
Jamaica
    13-19, 21, 25, 32, 39, 48, 63,
    64, 72, 77, 93, 96, 98
Johns Island
    73, 81, 93, 96, 97
Johnson, Charles
    25, 46,
Johnson, Nathaniel
    58–60, 64

## K
Kelly, James
    2, 7, 18, 19, 21–23, 89–93
Kiawah
    79–82, 88, 93–95, 97
Kidd, William
    61, 83, 90, 92

## L
Linckley, Christopher
    58, 70
Lowther
    86
*Loyal Jamaica*
    17-19, 21, 22, 44, 48, 51, 53,
    61-63, 65–68, 70-75, 82-85,
    87, 89, 91-94, 99

Ludwell, Philip
    53–56, 65, 83, 84, 114

## M
Madagascar
    24, 25, 32, 34–39, 41, 45–48,
    54, 62, 65, 67, 89–91, 94
Malagasy
    37, 39, 40, 45, 46
Maryland
    71, 83, 106, 107
St. Mary's
    40, 42, 44–46, 62, 90, 91, 94
Massachusetts
    13, 83, 99
Medlicott, Edmund
    58, 64, 65
Misroon House
    79
Mocha
    33, 34, 35, 90
Morgan, Henry
    14, 63
Mozambique
    24
Mughal
    2, 7, 24–29, 31, 34–36, 42,
    66, 67, 68, 72, 88, 103
Murrell's Inlet
    71

## N
Nairne, Thomas
    67
Nassau
    67
Newton, Richard
    58, 64

*Index*

## O
Old Chiswick Cemetery
76
Ottoman
22, 28–30
O'Brien, William
17

## P
Palmer, Joseph
58, 61
Philipse, Frederick
40
Thomas, Pierre
9, 16
Pinckney, Charles
58, 59, 64, 65, 74, 75
Pinckneyville
74
Port-de-Paix
13, 16, 17, 64, 65
Portsmouth
91
Privateer
11, 13-17, 16, 21, 22, 26, 51, 56, 57,   61, 63, 64, 66, 72, 77, 82, 85, 89, 91, 92

## R
Rackham, Jack (John)
86
Randolph, Edward
84, 109
Rawlins, Edward
58, 64
Rawlinson, Daniel
58

Raynor, Deborah
89
Raynor, Ebenezer
89
Raynor, Elias
70
Raynor, George
1, 7, 11, 16, 18, 19, 21, 24, 25–27, 29, 31, 32, 34, 36 40, 42, 44, 48, 53, 56, 58–65, 67–73, 76–83, 87–94 96, 97, 99–101
Raynor, Jessie
89
Raynor, Josiah
7, 26, 87–89, 99
Raynor, Uriah
88
Rhett, William
86
Rhode Island
26
Richardson, Adam
58, 60, 69
Risby
72, 73, 80
Roberts, Bartholomew
50
Rochelle
16, 44, 92
*HMS Roebuck*
49

## S
Sainte-Marie
39, 104
Santo Domingo
16, 102

123

Seabrooke, Robert
  63
Skroder, Peter
  48, 49, 54
Somalia
  24, 31, 32, 86
Sothel, Seth
  48, 51, 53, 54, 60, 61, 79, 82
Southampton
  88
St. Augustine
  60, 72, 80, 85, 88
St. Botolph
  76
Stono River
  73, 79, 97, 98
Suffolk
  88
Sullivan, John
  58
Sullivan's Island
  54
Surrat
  33, 34

# T
Teredo Worm
  43
Tew, Thomas
  24, 26, 40, 61, 72, 87, 88
Tomotley
  61
Tony
  97
Tortuga
  13, 14, 16
Turk
  35, 46, 96

# U
Uzbekistan
  27

# W
Wafer, Lional
  26, 91
Washington, George
  74
Wattkins, John
  58, 60
Want, Richard
  71, 72
Westminster
  76
Whydah
  24
Wilkes, Joshua
  58, 59
Williams, William
  58
Wilson, Ralph
  58
*Winchelsea*
  21
*Winchelsey*
  21
Worley, Richard
  86

# Y
Yemassee
  61
Yemen
  31
Yorkshire
  76

# ABOUT THE AUTHOR

Adam Morrow, alias Captain Marrow, is a pirate historian, reenactor, artist, photographer, and model. Originally from South Haven, Michigan, and growing up on the Great Lakes ever-enthralled by pirate media, his focus turned to history after relocating to the southeast Atlantic coast. For many years he has operated the pirate history page 'Shipwrecked with Captain Marrow' on Facebook, traveling the southeast shores investigating pirate lore and educating locals while on these endeavors, as well as partaking in public educational functions. He currently resides near the port of Charleston, South Carolina; a location rich in pirate history, that which was covered in this book and more. There, together with his partner Ava, they care for their family of rescue cats.

This book was a departure from Marrow's previous works, the 'Pirate Ghosts & Buried Treasures' series, which are compilations of historical dives into pirate folklore. For more published pirate history, consider checking out *Pirate Ghosts & Buried Treasures of the Southeast Coast: A Historical Assessment on Pirate Folklore*, and its follow-up, *Pirate Ghosts & Buried Treasures of the Northeast Coast*.

*Arabian Gold: Charleston's Red Sea Pirates of 1692*

Thank you for reading *Arabian Gold: Charleston's Red Sea Pirates of 1692 - Being the True Tale of Capt. George Raynor & the Crew of the Bachelor's Delight*

Please share your feedback, if you're so inclined, by posting on social media using the following hashtags and handles:

#arabiangold #captainmarrow, #shipwreckedwithcaptainmarrow
@shipwreckedwithcaptainmarrow

To book Captain Marrow for an educational or author event, online interviews, or just to contact, please reach out:

Facebook.com/shipwreckedwithcaptainmarrow2.0
Instagram.com/shipwreckedwithcaptainmarrow
Adamaro233@outlook.com

If you enjoyed this work of piratical history, please consider writing a review with your honest opinions on Goodreads, Amazon, or the platform of your choosing. Feedback such as this is incredibly valuable for assisting independent authors in reaching a wider audience.

To learn more about Captain Marrow and upcoming book releases outside of social media, please visit:

captainmarrowauthor.wixsite.com/captainmarrowauthor

Made in the USA
Columbia, SC
09 March 2025

54907117R00070